I0831070

Hemingway's SPANISH TABLE

A Culinary Journey in 60+ Recipes

Howie Southworth

weldonowen

Gratitude and Appreciation

For Jessica, Cooper, Griffin, and Greg.
For friends at my table, now and always.

&

For those who kept the place warm,
the glasses full, and the stories true:

The Westin Palace, Madrid

Restaurante Sobrino de Botín, Madrid

Pictura Bar, Mandarin Oriental Ritz, Madrid

El MiniBar, Madrid

Hotel Alfonso XIII, Sevilla

Restaurante Casa Cuesta, Triana, Sevilla

Restaurante Palo Cortao, Sevilla

Central Bar, Mercat Central, Valencia

Bar Cremaet, Valencia

Hotel La Perla, Pamplona

Restaurante BaserriBerri, Pamplona

Bar Gaucho, Pamplona

Hotel Avenida Palace, Barcelona

Bar del Pla, Barcelona

Restaurante Keik, Barcelona

LA CARTA

The Menu

This table of contents provides a menu in the style of a Spanish restaurant. From it, the home cook can create a meal of traditional courses that ranges from snacks and soups to desserts and drinks. Alternatively, the book and recipes can be consumed by following *El Viaje*, or The Journey, and retracing the footsteps the author took on his culinary journey through Spain.

FOREWORD BY SIMON MAJUMDAR 14
PREFACE 17
INTRODUCTION 18
HOW TO USE THIS BOOK 20
NOTES ABOUT SPANISH TECHNIQUES 22
SPECIALIZED SPANISH INGREDIENTS 25
HEMINGWAY'S SPAIN 26
CULINARY HIGHLIGHTS 27

PICA PICA
Snacks

Queso Manchego con Avellanas 40
Manchego Cheese with Honey and Hazelnuts

Chorizo al Vino 43
Red Wine Chorizo

Tapa Bretón 54
Roasted Goat Cheese

Espinacas con Garbanzos 77
Spinach and Chickpeas

Tartar de Toro con Tuetano 92
Beef Tartare with Bone Marrow

Pimientos del Padrón Fritos 97
Blistered Padrón Peppers

Gambas al Ajillo 98
Sizzling Garlic Shrimp

Tataki de Atún 106
Seared Ahi Tuna

Albóndigas al Curry Rojo 120
Meatballs in Red Curry

Pimientos Rellenos 127
Stuffed Roasted Peppers

Mojama con Cebollas Encurtidas 155
Salt-Cured Tuna and Pickled Onions

Galletas de Socarrat 189
Crispy Rice Cookies

Tatin de Rabo de Buey 191
Oxtail Puff Pastry

FRITURAS
Fried Snacks

Croquetas de Jamón 47
Ham Croquettes

Berenjenas con Miel de Caña 74
Fried Eggplant with Molasses

Flamenquín 78
Chicken Roulade

Langostino Wonton 186
Fried Shrimp in Noodles

ENSALADAS Y SOPAS
Salads and Soups

Sopa de Ajo 35
Garlic Soup

Tomates Aliñados 57
Dressed Tomatoes

Gazpacho 67
Chilled Vegetable Soup

Papas Aliñadas 72
Potato Salad

Salmorejo 85
Chilled Tomato Soup

Ajo Blanco 95
Chilled White Garlic Soup

Ensaladilla de Alubias 148
White Bean Salad

Ensalada de Perdiz Escabechada 180
Poached Partridge with Salad

ENTREPANES Y PINTXOS
Sandwiches and Canapés

Bocadillo de Calamares 36
Fried Squid Sandwich

Pan con Tomate........ 81
Toast with Tomato Smear

Bocadillo de Morcilla y Revueltos 122
Black Sausage and Egg Sandwich

Coca de Berenjena y Tomate 132
Tomato and Eggplant Flatbread

El Chivito 135
Pork, Bacon, and Egg Sandwich

Empanadilla de Atún 136
Tuna Turnover

Pintxo de Anguila y Tomate 156
Eel and Tomato Canapé

bOOmVeja! Pintxo de Cordero 158
Shredded Lamb Canapé

Tosta con Mantequilla y Mermelada 162
Raspberry Jam on Toast

Pintxo de Gilda........ 178
Skewer of Olive, Pepper, and Anchovy

HUEVOS
Eggs

Tortilla Española de Patatas 50
Spanish Potato Tortilla

Migas de Pastor con Chistorra 143
Breadcrumbs, Fried Egg, and Sausage

Huevo Trufado 153
Truffled Egg

Revueltos de Hongos........ 179
Scrambled Eggs with Mushrooms

Tortilla Vaga de Bacalao........ 188
Salt-Cod "Lazy" Spanish Tortilla

CARNES
Meats

Cochinillo Asado con Patatas Asadas 32
Roasted Suckling Pig and Potatoes

Confit de Pato Glaseado 59
Glazed Duck Confit

Rabo de Toro........ 62
Braised Oxtail

Solomillo al Whiskey........ 75
Pork Tenderloin with Whiskey Sauce

Chuletas de Cordero a la Parrilla........ 101
Grilled Lamb Chops

Lomo Alto a la Parrilla 168
Grilled New York Strip Steak

Carrilleras con Pimientos Cristal 177
Braised Pork Cheeks and Peppers

PESCADOS Y MARISCOS
Fish and Seafood

Bacalao con Tomate........ 89
Salt-Cod in Tomato Sauce

Almejas con Chorizo 112
Clams with Sausage

Trucha Ahumada 147
Smoked Trout

Salmón con Salsa Béarnaise 163
Broiled Salmon with Béarnaise Sauce

ARROCES Y FIDEUAS
Rices and Noodles

Paella Valenciana 109
Chicken and Rabbit Rice

Arróz del Senyoret con Salmonete 114
Naked Seafood and Fish Rice

Arróz de Vaca Madurada 128
Dry-Aged Beef Rice

VERDURAS
Vegetables

Hongos de Temporada y Yema 44
Seasonal Mushrooms with Egg Yolk

Alcachofas Parrilladas 69
Grilled Artichokes

Pimientos del Piquillo Confitados 111
Charred Roasted Peppers

Berenjenas con Soja y Miso 119
Eggplant with Soy and Miso

Patatas a la Riojana 165
Rioja Potato Stew

Patatas Bravas 171
Roasted Potatoes with "Brave" Sauce

Pisto 174
Ratatouille

BEBIDAS
Beverages

Papa Doble 41
Hemingway Daiquiri

Tinto de Verano 56
Red Wine Spritzer

Sangría 110
Fruit-Infused Wine

Cremaet 123
Burnt Rum Coffee

Horchata 133
Chilled Tiger-Nut Milk

Vermút Casera 145
House-Made Fortified Wine

POSTRES
Desserts

Tarta de Santiago 33
Almond Flour Cake

Torrijas 86
French Toast

Tarta de Queso 183
Basque "Burnt" Cheesecake

AN EXPLANATORY GLOSSARY OF CERTAIN WORDS, TERMS, AND PHRASES 192

ERNEST HEMINGWAY'S SPAIN, A TIMELINE 193

INDEX 194

EL VIAJE

The Journey

This book takes the reader on a culinary adventure through Spain that connects Hemingway and his writings to the featured foods. It is divided into parts, each of which focuses on a city or region. The chapters within tell the individual stories of eating and drinking across the country, with relevant recipes following chapter introductions.

Part I: MADRID

Chapter 1
CAPITAL OF THE WORLD: THE ESSENCE OF SPAIN 30

Cochinillo Asado con Patatas Asadas
Roasted Suckling Pig and Potatoes 32

Tarta de Santiago
Almond Flour Cake 33

Sopa de Ajo
Garlic Soup 35

Bocadillo de Calamares
Fried Squid Sandwich 36

Chapter 2
SIMPLE, HONEST, ROBUST: AS FOOD SHOULD BE 38

Queso Manchego con Miel y Avellanas
Manchego Cheese with Honey and Hazelnuts 40

Papa Doble
Hemingway Daiquiri 41

Chorizo al Vino
Red Wine Chorizo 43

Hongos de Temporada y Yema
Seasonal Mushrooms with Egg Yolk 44

Croquetas de Jamón
Ham Croquettes 47

Chapter 3
MORNING WALK: THE PARK 48

Tortilla Española de Patatas
Spanish Potato Tortilla 50

Chapter 4
THE ARTS: A DISH IS WORTH A THOUSAND WORDS 52

Tapa Bretón
Roasted Goat Cheese 54

Tinto de Verano
Red Wine Spritzer 56

Tomates Aliñados
Dressed Tomatoes 57

Confit de Pato Glaseado
Glazed Duck Confit 59

Chapter 5
THE BULL: AFICIONADO HEMINGWAY 60

Rabo de Toro
Braised Oxtail 62

Part II: SEVILLA

Chapter 6
COMFORTLESS GRANDEUR: A CITY OF MIXED FEELINGS 66

Gazpacho
Chilled Vegetable Soup 67

Alcachofas Parrilladas
Grilled Artichokes 69

Chapter 7
CAMARADERIE: TAPAS IN GOOD COMPANY 70

Papas Aliñadas
Potato Salad 72

Berenjenas con Miel de Caña
Fried Eggplant with Molasses 74

Solomillo al Whiskey
Pork Tenderloin with Whiskey Sauce 75

Espinacas con Garbanzos
Spinach and Chickpeas 77

Flamenquín
Chicken Roulade 78

Chapter 8
MORNING WALK:
THE PEOPLE'S BREAKFAST 80

Pan con Tomate
Toast with Tomato Smear 81

Chapter 9
THE PASSION: ONE HOLY MEAL 82

Salmorejo
Chilled Tomato Soup 85

Torrijas
French Toast 86

Bacalao con Tomate
Salt-Cod in Tomato Sauce 89

Chapter 10
THE BULL: A VIP DINNER 90

Tartar de Toro con Tuetano
Beef Tartare with Bone Marrow 92

Ajo Blanco
Chilled White Garlic Soup 95

Chapter 11
ROMANCE: RONDA SIZZLES 96

Pimientos del Padrón Fritos
Blistered Padrón Peppers 97

Gambas al Ajillo
Sizzling Garlic Shrimp 98

Chuletas de Cordero a la Parrilla
Grilled Lamb Chops 101

Part III: VALENCIA

Chapter 12
THE SEA: PAELLA AND BEYOND 104

Tataki de Atún
Seared Ahi Tuna 106

Paella Valenciana
Chicken and Rabbit Rice 109

Sangría
Fruit-Infused Wine 110

Pimientos del Piquillo Confitados
Charred Roasted Peppers 111

Almejas con Chorizo
Clams with Sausage 112

Arróz del Senyoret con Salmonete
Naked Seafood and Fish Rice 114

Chapter 13
THE LAND:
A VISIT TO CENTRAL MARKET 116

Berenjenas con Soja y Miso
Eggplant with Soy and Miso 119

Albóndigas al Curry Rojo
Meatballs in Red Curry 120

Bocadillo de Morcilla y Revueltos
Black Sausage and Egg Sandwich 122

Cremaet
Burnt Rum Coffee 123

Chapter 14
THE BULL: OF SWORDS AND RICE 124

Pimientos Rellenos
Stuffed Roasted Peppers 127

Arróz de Vaca Madurada
Dry-Aged Beef Rice 128

Chapter 15
MORNING WALK: THE BREAD OF WAR 130

Coca de Berenjena y Tomate
Tomato and Eggplant Flatbread 132

Horchata
Chilled Tiger-Nut Milk 133

El Chivito
Pork, Bacon, and Egg Sandwich 135

Empanadilla de Atún
Tuna Turnover 136

Part IV: PAMPLONA

Chapter 16

ARRIVAL AND MORNING WALK: WELCOME HOME **140**

Migas de Pastor con Chistorra
Breadcrumbs, Fried Egg, and Sausage 143

Vermút Casera
House-Made Fortified Wine 145

Chapter 17

THE COUNTRYSIDE: CALL OF THE MOUNTAINS **146**

Trucha Ahumada
Smoked Trout 147

Ensaladilla de Alubias
White Bean Salad 148

Chapter 18

FIESTA DE SAN FERMÍN: A VERY HEMINGWAY PARTY **150**

Huevo Trufado
Truffled Egg 153

Mojama con Cebollas Encurtidas
Salt-Cured Tuna and Pickled Onions 155

Pintxo de Anguila y Tomate
Eel and Tomato Canapé 156

bOOmVeja! Pintxo de Cordero
Shredded Lamb Canapé 158

Chapter 19

MORNING WALK AND A SWIM: THE PARTY'S OVER **160**

Tosta con Mantequilla y Mermelada
Raspberry Jam on Toast 162

Salmón con Salsa Béarnaise
Broiled Salmon with Béarnaise Sauce 163

Patatas a la Riojana
Rioja Potato Stew 165

Chapter 20

THE BULL: HEMINGWAY'S ENCIERRO **166**

Lomo Alto a la Parrilla
Grilled New York Strip Steak 168

Patatas Bravas
Roasted Potatoes with "Brave" Sauce 171

Chapter 21

THE FIRST MEAL IN SPAIN **172**

Pisto
Ratatouille 174

Carrilleras con Pimientos Cristal
Braised Pork Cheeks and Peppers 177

Pintxo de Gilda
Skewer of Olive, Pepper, and Anchovy 178

Revueltos de Hongos
Scrambled Eggs with Mushrooms 179

Ensalada de Perdiz Escabechada
Poached Partridge with Salad 180

Tarta de Queso
Basque "Burnt" Cheesecake 183

Epilogue

BARCELONA **184**

Langostino Wonton
Fried Shrimp in Noodles 186

Tortilla Vaga de Bacalao
Salt-Cod "Lazy" Spanish Tortilla 188

Galletas de Socarrat
Crispy Rice Cookies 189

Tatin de Rabo de Buey
Oxtail Puff Pastry 191

FOREWORD

by Simon Majumdar

There is no circumstance in which I am comparing my measly little writings to Ernest Hemingway's. There are, however, two circumstances where I could easily imagine myself following his colossal steps as he walked around Spain, an extraordinary and elegant country.

The first circumstance would be his own vibrant passion for exploring this country. I have been to Spain close to a hundred times. I have visited every state—from Andalusia to Aragon, from the Basque Country to Castile and León, and from Catalonia to Extremadura—and enjoyed their different climates, geography, and local culture. Even now, as I write this from Los Angeles, those names make me desperate to visit them all again.

The second circumstance, and the reason I visited them in the first place, would be the food. Love of food is something where I might get close—very close—to Hemingway's obsession with what the Spanish ate and drank. After all, a racion of Jamón Ibérico Gran Reserva from Extremadura goes perfectly well with a glass of Ribera del Duero from Castile and León. Fresh *gambas* from the southern coast of Andalusia pairs wonderfully with a glass of Manzanilla sherry from Jerez. And, paella from Valencia—maybe with chicken or rabbit, the original style of paella—magically tastes even better with, dare I say, vermouth. One can easily enjoy the simple pleasures in life just by having a bite of *pan con tomate* while standing up at a tapas bar. Or perhaps pleasure may be found while having a small beer or *caña* at someone's home while getting ready to go out at ten p.m. to be a part of the throngs of people on the streets thinking about dinner, going to dinner, or having dinner.

Hemingway wrote rich, vivid, and stirring stories of his time in Spain. His tales about this country, including the running of the bulls during the Festival of San Fermín in *The Sun Also Rises*, and the Spanish Civil War and the bloody battles he saw in *For Whom the Bell Tolls*, won him much literary acclaim. But, I have no doubt that "Papa" would have won even more accolades if he simply focused his writing on his own obsession with the food of Spain.

Which is why I was so thrilled to be asked to pen this foreword for another Spain-ophile and another Ernest-ophile: Howie Southworth.

In his book, *Hemingway's Spanish Table*, Southworth dreamed of following Hemingway's food passage around Spain. As he follows Hemingway's journey from Madrid to Sevilla to Valencia to Pamplona and then to Barcelona, or as he calls it, "Spain not Spain," Southworth finds Hemingway to be a vital guide.

Southworth is an academic about Hemingway. *Hemingway's Spanish Table* is filled to the brim with stories taken from many letters and, of course, the books that made him so famous, such as *The Dangerous Summer*, *For Whom the Bell Tolls*, *Death in the Afternoon*, or my own favorite, *The Sun Also Rises*. But *Hemingway's Spanish Table* is also filled with the same fervor for Spain and its food, just like Hemingway.

Hemingway's Spanish Table is a cookbook that highlights Hemingway's Spain with more than sixty recipes that make me feel hungry for the food and the country. It is filled with recipes that make me need to be back there again. And thanks to recipes like *Cochinillo Asado con Patatas Asadas* (Roasted Suckling Pig and Potatoes, page 32), *Croquetas de Jamón* (Ham Croquettes, page 47), and *Pan con Tomate* (page 81), which Southworth rather endearingly calls "Toast with Tomato Smear," I feel that my kitchen can bring me back to Spain.

Hemingway's Spanish Table is also Southworth's love letter to his own visits to this remarkable country filled with his own joy of visiting these amazing cities.

Also, I think it is the sort of book Hemingway would have approved of.

Whatever this book is to you, sit down, have a glass of Ribeiro del Duero, have a bite of Cochinillo Asado, and enjoy *El Viaje*.

Simon Majumdar
Author of *Eat My Globe* and *Fed, White, and Blue*
(Los Angeles)

PREFACE

When I first learned I'd be moving to Spain, I had no great anticipation. No daydreams of sipping vermouth in tiled courtyards. No imagined strolls past *jamón* legs hanging in market stalls. In fact, I had barely thought about Spain at all. Not its people, its politics, or—most surprisingly—its cuisine.

This admission might seem odd in the preface to a Spanish cookbook, but it's the truth. My obsessions had long been aimed elsewhere: East Asia, mostly, with its layered histories and bold flavors. Spain never even made the short list. So when my wife, Jessica, received a work assignment in Barcelona in 2017, I was proud of her. I was excited for the adventure, but I otherwise drew a blank. Still, I'm wired to find a hook. And food has always been mine. So I did what I always do before landing in a new country: I started searching for what to eat.

The first returns were not inspiring. A handful of tired top-ten lists played out the usual suspects—paella, *jamón*, tortilla, gazpacho, *pan con tomate*. None of it seemed, well, electric. It wasn't until I put the clickbait away and returned to the page—books, essays, and most notably, Hemingway—that the engine started. Not with fireworks, but with flint.

Hemingway, I found, understood Spain differently. He saw its food not as a parade of dishes, but as a language. A way to access its passions, rituals, and truths. In *The Sun Also Rises*, his characters dine with purpose and drink with pleasure. In *Death in the Afternoon*, he explores the country through bullfights and the interstitial meals. In *For Whom the Bell Tolls*, food is life. Even when he doesn't title the dishes, you feel the plates on the table: the garlic, the broth, the heat, the pride.

Then, my travels through Spain began to mimic his own. In Madrid, I found the taverns he loved, where suckling pig still arrives crisp and blistered. In Valencia, I pursued the rice dishes he never quite named but surely knew. In Sevilla, I let his ambivalence about the city inform my own nights among the sherry drinkers and bullfight skeptics. In Pamplona, I partied. I ate and read and walked and asked questions.

What began as a casual search became something closer to a fixation. One that grew more specific: not just Spanish food, but Hemingway's Spanish Table—real or inspired, remembered or roused.

This book is the product of that curiosity. It is not a traditional cookbook, nor is it a literary analysis with side dishes. It is a travelogue through food, a cultural excavation, and a companionable romp through the dishes that defined a country and shaped a writer. It is equal parts history, hunger, and homage.

I cooked from memories. I cooked from menus. I cooked to bring Spain home. And I wrote to bring Hemingway's love for the country into focus—not through the lens of war or masculinity, horns or mythmaking, but through meals. Because that's where Spain reveals itself: in the olive oil pooled on the crumb of bread, in the patience of slowly braised meat, in the clink of a glass raised at sunset. Hemingway knew that. Eventually, so did I.

And now, I hope you will too.

INTRODUCTION

"... the country that I loved more than any other except my own ..."

—*The Dangerous Summer*

Ernest Hemingway loved Spain like a man loves a place that made him whole. It was not merely the country of bullfights and fiestas, though these captivated him. For Hemingway, Spain was a place where life's beauty and brutality intertwined in ways he found compelling. Along with his journalism during the Spanish Civil War, several short stories, and a play, Hemingway wrote of Spain in his books:

- *The Sun Also Rises*: Reporter Jake Barnes and his band of disillusioned expatriates navigate friendship, festivity, and life's meaning with a backdrop of post–World War I France and Spain.
- *For Whom the Bell Tolls*: American munitions expert Robert Jordan grapples with loyalty, romance, and unconditional sacrifice during the Spanish Civil War.
- *Death in the Afternoon*: Hemingway explores the tragedy and art of Spanish bullfighting through mechanics, philosophy, humor, and reflection.
- *The Dangerous Summer*: Hemingway follows a season-long rivalry between two prominent matadors through Spain in 1959, including travels outside of the bullring.

On writing, Hemingway said, "All good books have one thing in common, they are truer than if they had really happened, and after you've read one of them you will feel that all that happened, happened to you and then it belongs to you forever: the happiness and unhappiness, good and evil, ecstasy and sorrow, the food, wine, beds, people and the weather. If you can give that to readers, then you're a writer." And give it, he did. These stories and books weren't just chronicles set in Spain. They *were* Spain. He saw in it a reflection of himself, a land of contradictions, where joy and tragedy danced as one. Through his words, he touched the beating heart of its people, the luminance of its culture, and the traditions that bound it all together. He found its essence in its passions, bullfighting, arts, and food.

Spain's cuisine, like the bullfight, was more than lifeblood for Hemingway. It was a doorway into Spain's soul, a way to understand its rituals and its humanity. In Spanish food, he discovered honesty, meals made with simple ingredients but prepared with pride and precision. He saw how food turned strangers into friends, how a shared plate of ham or a bottle of wine could amplify a quiet evening into something memorable. Hemingway's characters dined with intention, as did he, not simply to eat but to bond, to a place, to a moment, to each other. Spain's restaurants and bars, like its bullrings, were where he felt life most keenly, and they became as much a part of his writing as winding alleyways or the cheers for a matador's pass.

Hemingway's Spanish Table is a journey inspired by giant footsteps from storied taverns in Madrid and proletariat counters in Sevilla to seaside feasts in Valencia and wild celebrations in Pamplona. "Don't bother with churches, government buildings or city squares," he advised. "If you want to know about a culture, spend a night in its bars." We follow that call. Within these pages, you'll find gastronomic adventures along his well-marked routes and into hidden corners, very much in his spirit of discovery. In Hemingway's haunts and modern places where he'd fit right in, we indulge in delicious experiences, emblematic drinks, scenic walks, and revelry, all of which deepened his love for Spain.

The foods he named outright in his works are easy enough to find, like suckling pig or trout in *The Sun Also Rises*. The quotes above many recipes in this book tell the tale. But it's the others, the ones you taste in his settings, feel in his wanderings, imagine in his silences, the ones he could never refuse, that linger. These are the treasures hidden beneath the visible part of the iceberg. *Pintxos*, for instance, he never mentioned by name, though they loom over every page set in the Basque country. Hemingway used food both explicitly and implicitly to propel his characters forward, to connect them, to mark a celebration or a pause, to illuminate Spain. We follow his lead, through nights of tapas, leisurely multicourse meals, quick nibbles on the go, mornings with coffee and light fare, and moments honoring the sacrifice of a bull.

The *El Viaje* table of contents mirrors our journey, unfolding through Madrid, Sevilla, Ronda, Valencia, and Pamplona, with an epilogue in Barcelona. From the magnificence of Spain's capital to the exuberance of Basque Country, the chapters within each place tell our tales of food and drink. Every tale relates to an aspect of Spanish culture that called to Hemingway, be it the arts, camaraderie, the sea, festivity, or passion, all followed by the right and faithful recipes. But take note, in the case of a plate of *jamón*, a selection of cheeses, or another uncomplicated bite, a recipe may be overkill and therefore skipped.

Our outings may not follow one's expected meal of an appetizer, main, and dessert, but rather a moveable feast, a snack with a drink or four, the way Hemingway would have had it. It is a cross-country culinary expedition with stops for decadent Spanish tortilla, refreshing gazpacho, creamy

Basque cheesecake, jolting *café bombón*, and sizzling paella, to mention a few. But this is more than a cookbook. To read it like a novel would be to honor Hemingway's spirit. Still, we've included the *La Carta* table of contents as well, a menu akin to what you'd find at a Spanish restaurant. With page numbers instead of prices, it organizes recipes into courses so you can create a meal to share with friends before diving back into the stories.

This book is not just a culinary guide; it is a love letter to Spain. Through the journey, we share Hemingway's discovery of a land where food was never merely about sustenance, but about life itself. Each story evokes a moment, and each recipe invites you to join it. Whether you come for the lore, the dishes, or simply to imagine yourself at Hemingway's table, we hope this book leaves you with a hunger for the country that inspired one of the greatest writers of the twentieth century.

HOW TO USE THIS BOOK

Welcome to *Hemingway's Spanish Table* and a gastronomic journey that follows in Papa's footsteps through Spain. This book is organized a bit differently from traditional cookbooks and highlights both Spanish culinary traditions as well as the narrative adventure of eating and drinking in some of his favorite places on Earth.

Book Structure

PARTS: The book is divided into five parts, each a stop along our path of Hemingway's most prominent Spanish destinations. This path is not necessarily the order in which Hemingway traveled, but each destination helped build his Spanish story.

- Part I: Madrid—the capital of the world, as Hemingway would have it
- Part II: Sevilla—the traditional soul of Spain, and a place of some consternation
- Part III: Valencia—Hemingway's retreat, where land meets the sea
- Part IV: Pamplona—where Hemingway's Spanish love affair began
- Epilogue: Barcelona—Spain, but not Spanish?

CHAPTERS: Each part includes thematic chapters that explore aspects of Spanish culture that inspired Hemingway's work. Be it passion, bullfighting, the arts, camaraderie, festivals, history, or simply food, the chapters tell tales of our journey where Hemingway looms heavy and points the way.

RECIPES: Each chapter introduction is followed by select recipes from that adventure. Not every food we consumed is accompanied by a recipe, but if it has some level of complexity, uniqueness, or cultural interest, it's in there. All recipes are adapted for the home kitchen, but each is true to Spanish techniques.

Navigation Features

CROSS-REFERENCES: When a given recipe uses a sauce or other preparation from another recipe, a page reference will guide the reader to the necessary process or ingredients.

HEMINGWAY QUOTES: Atop each chapter introduction and ahead of each recipe lie quotes from Hemingway's writings. Each quote offers a reason why an ingredient, a method, or even a full dish was included in the book. At times, the quote is simply fun and apropos.

COLOR COMMENTARY: Also at the start of each recipe is an interesting bit about the dish, an ingredient, or pertinent trivia about Spanish gastronomy. In some special cases, we recount conversations with restaurant owners and chefs about recipes they've graciously contributed to the book.

Suggested Pathways Through the Book

FOR THE LITERARY ENTHUSIAST: Read and cook from the book following the table of contents labeled *El Viaje*, The Journey. This pathway takes readers on a culinary adventure through Spain connecting Hemingway and his writings to the food. Each part is a setting in which the chapters tell our stories of eating and drinking across the country. Relevant recipes follow each chapter introduction.

FOR THE MEAL PLANNER: Peruse the table of contents, labeled *La Carta*, The Menu, and put together a balanced Spanish meal. *La Carta* is a menu in the style of a Spanish restaurant. From it, the home cook can compile a feast of traditional courses, from snacks and soups to desserts and drinks. Then visit *El Viaje* for pure reading pleasure.

NOTES ABOUT SPANISH TECHNIQUES

Bacalao

The Basque method of salt-preserving cod has sustained Europe for centuries and provides a durable, economical source of protein. This enduring practice is still widely used throughout Spain today, and *bacalao* is nearly universal on Spanish menus. It frequently plays a starring role in *croquetas*, tortillas, spreads, salads, or as fillets. The trick to using it is first ridding the fish of all that salt. Soaking it for 24 to 48 hours with a few changes of the water is necessary before portioning and cooking. In a European supermarket, de-salted *bacalao* is readily available, as is the still-crusted product. In a pinch, it's fine to substitute fresh or defrosted cod and salt it for a few hours before cooking, although be aware that the texture will not match the level of meatiness of true *bacalao*.

Other Fish and Seafood

In a practice that seems counterintuitive in an American kitchen, Spanish recipes often feature fish and seafood that is cooked from room temperature, rather than direct from refrigeration. When relatively delicate aquatic muscles seize up due to a large temperature swing, e.g., from refrigeration at about 37°F to hot oil of 350°F, the result can be fish with a tough texture. Not in Spain, where oceanic and terrestrial meats are allowed to rest at about 70°F for up to 2 hours before facing the fire. Spain is also the land of canned fish and seafood, and the quality of the protein is often higher than fresh or frozen, and it's already cooked. To take the guesswork out of dishes like seafood paella, one option is to add canned specimens at the very end, assuming the rice is cooked in an otherwise-prepared seafood stock.

Paella

Paella proper is one very specific example within scores of Spanish rice dishes. On a restaurant menu, formal options may include *Paella Valenciana* (page 109) and *paella de mariscos*. The first, named to honor Valencia, the place of paella's birth, is a mix of rice, poultry, rabbit, beans, and sometimes snails or seasonal artichokes. The second is topped with sundry seafood, based on the aquatic ways of coastal Valencia. The *paellera* or paella pan is shallow and wide, encouraging the bottom rice to toast into a thin, crispy layer, or *socarrat*. A cast-iron skillet can yield similar results. Though paella is Spain's "national dish," Valencia remains special for the purity and pride in the dish. Dishes on a restaurant menu similar to paella but not so specific may be titled *arróz seco* (dry rice with other starring ingredients). There may also be *arróz meloso* (creamy rice) and *arróz caldoso* (soupy rice). None of these are paella.

Tapas

Tapas immediately come to mind when thinking about Spanish cuisine. They are often thought of as a singular thing or as a course unto themselves. But in Spain, a restaurant menu may or may not list "tapas" by this title. Some restaurants offer to serve many of their popular dishes as a tapa, on a small plate, portioned for easy sharing at the table. The casual style of eating tapas, or *tapeo*, typically considers the *whole* menu. A croquette or two, a scoop of potato salad, a few wooden spoons of paella, a slice of grilled bread topped with tomato, a wedge of tortilla, or even some almond cake. Courses be damned. Nearing the northeast of Spain, one is likely to see the word *pintxos* in place of "tapas," although, technically, a *pintxo* is a morsel of skewered food.

Tomatoes

The use of tomatoes is almost global, but few places outside of Spain *grate* their tomatoes for toast, stews, soups, and sauces. On the face of it, grating tomato flesh and discarding the skin seems improbable. But slicing the fruit in half and grating over a box grater, in the same way as shredding cheese, leads to textbook paella, tomato bread, or oxtail stew. The trick is pressing gently on the middle of the domed skin side while grating, and the skin will naturally push away from the grater. A food mill will also, generally, get rid of the skins. One rare use of tomatoes with their skins on in Spain is in salads, typically reserved for late summer, when the whole fruit is at its finest. Sliced tomato on Spanish sandwiches is virtually unheard of, though grated tomato with olive oil and salt is a common condiment.

Tortilla Española

Spanish tortilla is much like an Italian frittata or French omelet in the initial technique. But where a frittata sets on the bottom and then oven-roasts for a moment and an omelet sets on the bottom and then rolls onto a plate, a tortilla is flipped to finish. The flip may seem intimidating, but it can be accomplished with practice and a plate. A plate that is slightly larger than the skillet is placed upside down over the eggs, then the skillet and the plate are turned over in one move. The tortilla is then slid off the plate back into the skillet to finish cooking. The standard tortilla consists of eggs, potatoes, and, arguably, onions. Regionally, tortillas can vary in ingredients and final texture of the interior. In Madrid, for example, a perfect tortilla is almost runny in the middle, whereas in Barcelona, it is likely solid throughout.

CONSUMIX
PRODUCTE LOCAL
MER
CAT
CENTRAL
CONSUMIX
PRODUCTE LOCAL

SPECIALIZED SPANISH INGREDIENTS

English	Ingredient	Description	Substitution
Saffron	*Azafrán*	Threads of stigma and styles from the crocus flower	Ground turmeric; less floral and aromatic
Smoked paprika	*Pimentón dulce*	Smoked, dried, and ground mild red chiles	Chile powder, ground from a single type of chile; not spicy
Piquillo peppers	*Pimientos del piquillo*	Beak-shaped sweet red peppers, roasted, peeled, and jarred	Roasted and peeled red bell peppers; typically 1 equals 3 *piquillos*
Padrón peppers	*Pimientos del padrón*	Small green peppers that can be spicy or mild	Shishito peppers; slightly thinner
Bomba rice	*Arróz bomba*	Round, medium-grain rice from Valencia	Arborio or "risotto" rice; takes less water to cook
Aioli	*Alioli*	Egg and oil emulsion, which may contain garlic	Mayonnaise puréed with garlic and lemon juice
Extra-virgin olive oil	*Aceite de oliva*	Top-quality olive oil, made by cold-pressing without raising the temperature	Walnut oil or avocado oil; less fruity aroma and flavor
Salt-cod	*Bacalao*	Salt-cured cod that requires long water-soaking, then cooking	Fresh cod, salted for a few hours and rinsed; less meaty
Spanish ham	*Jamón*	Specifically, *Serrano* or *Iberérico* pork hams	Lean prosciutto, Parma ham, or Virginia country ham
Chistorra	*Chistorra*	Semi-cured, garlic- and paprika-spiced pork sausage	Mild *andouille* or kielbasa sausage; less paprika-forward
Blood sausage	*Morcilla*	Semi-cured pork sausage that includes blood	*Boudin noir*, *blutwurst*, black pudding; less paprika-forward
Spanish chorizo	*Chorizo*	Cured and dried, garlic- and paprika-spiced sausage	Mild *andouille* or kielbasa sausage; less paprika-forward
Rabbit meat	*Conejo*	Typically, the loin and legs, light and dark meat, respectively	Chicken breast and thigh meat; less gamey
Beef or pork cheeks	*Carrilleras*	Jowls and cheek meat from pigs and cattle	Pork shoulder or beef brisket; less even marbling
Suckling pig	*Cochinillo*	Typically, the whole young pig still feeding on milk	Pork belly; less tender, takes longer to cook
Partridge	*Perdiz*	Meat from the partridge bird	Cornish game hen

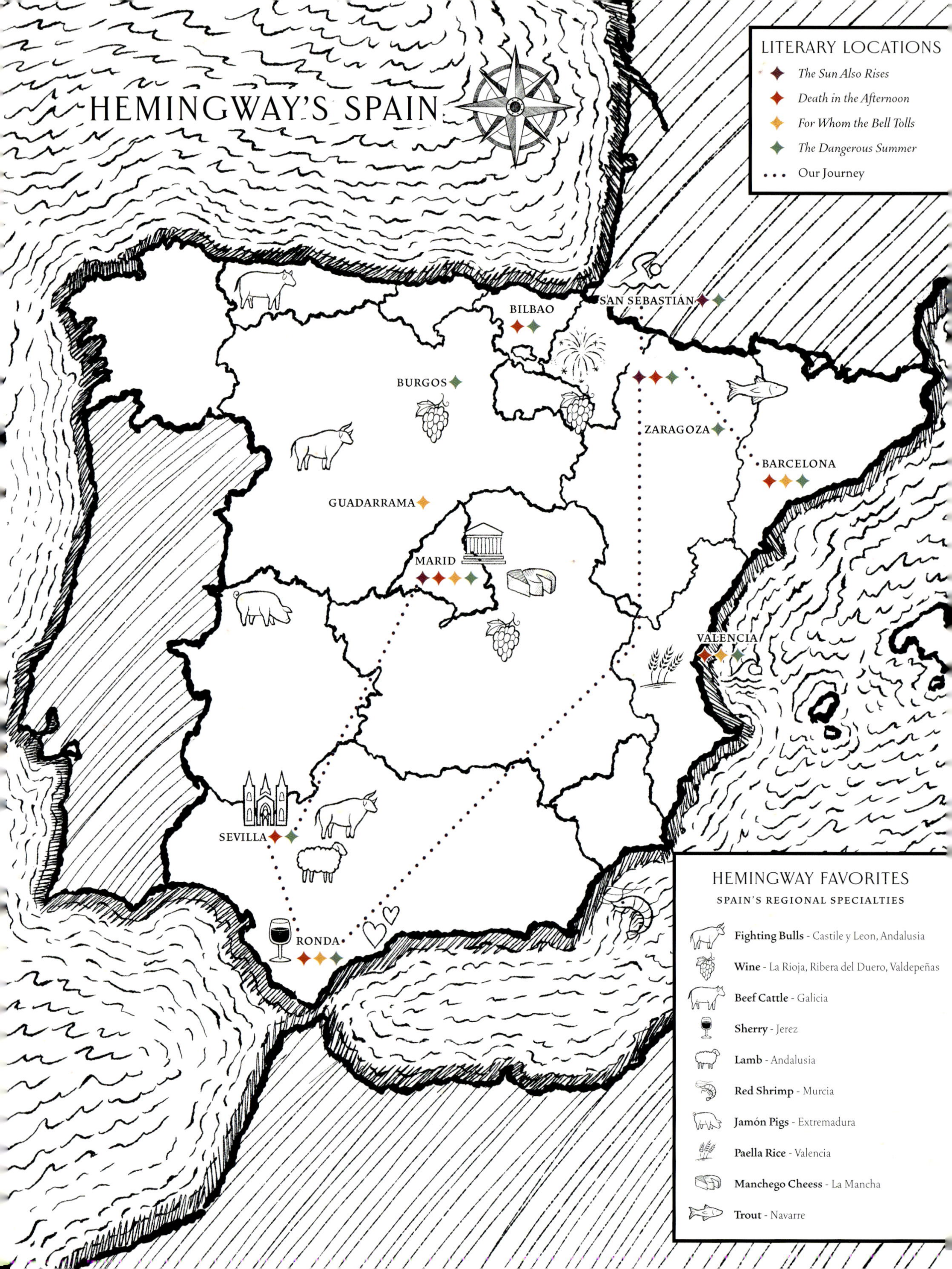
HEMINGWAY'S SPAIN
LITERARY LOCATIONS
The Sun Also Rises
Death in the Afternoon
For Whom the Bell Tolls
The Dangerous Summer
Our Journey
SAN SEBASTIÁN
BILBAO
BURGOS
ZARAGOZA
BARCELONA
GUADARRAMA
MARID
VALENCIA
SEVILLA
RONDA
HEMINGWAY FAVORITES
SPAIN'S REGIONAL SPECIALTIES
Fighting Bulls - Castile y Leon, Andalusia
Wine - La Rioja, Ribera del Duero, Valdepeñas
Beef Cattle - Galicia
Sherry - Jerez
Lamb - Andalusia
Red Shrimp - Murcia
Jamón Pigs - Extremadura
Paella Rice - Valencia
Manchego Cheess - La Mancha
Trout - Navarre

CULINARY HIGHLIGHTS

Madrid

Cochinillo Asado con Patatas Asadas—page 32

Croquetas de Jamón—page 47

Tortilla Española de Patatas—page 50

Rabo de Toro—page 62

Sevilla

Gazpacho—page 67

Solomillo al Whiskey—page 75

Torrijas—page 86

Ajo Blanco—page 95

Ronda

Chuletas de Cordero a la Parrilla—page 101

Valencia

Paella Valenciana—page 109

Pimientos Rellenos—page 127

Coca de Berenjena—page 132

El Chivito—page 135

Pamplona

Migas de Pastor—page 143

Trucha Ahumada—page 147

Huevo Trufado—page 153

Pintxo de Gilda—page 178

San Sebastián

Salmón con Salsa Béarnaise—page 163

Barcelona

Tortilla Vaga—page 188

Galletas de Socarrat—page 189

Literary Locations

The Sun Also Rises

Death in the Afternoon

For Whom the Bell Tolls

The Dangerous Summer

Our Journey

Part 1
MADRID

CHAPTER 1

CAPITAL OF THE WORLD

The Essence of Spain

"Madrid is a strange place anyway. I do not believe anyone likes it much when he first goes there. It has none of the look that you expect of Spain. It is modern rather than picturesque . . . Yet when you get to know it, it is the most Spanish of all cities, the best to live in, the finest people, month in and month out the finest climate . . . It is in Madrid only that you get the essence."

—*Death in the Afternoon*

Madrid is many things to many people. For Hemingway, Madrid held the best of Spain. It's a city that spoke to him through its food and drink. And bulls, but we'll get to that in time. Here we begin our gastronomic journey and indulge in classics that nourished a writer's soul. A nod to our final glimpse of Jake Barnes and Brett Ashley in *The Sun Also Rises,* we head straight to lunch at Hemingway's beating heart, Sobrino de Botín.

The antique wooden door swings open to reveal history, a restaurant where time stands still, but for the smartphones consuming the plates in photos before the first taste. It's old, some three hundred years of formally dressed waiters scuffing pathways onto the floor, delivering hearty *Madrileño* recipes that haven't changed in nearly as long. There's just something about dark wood and low ceilings that seems to amplify the aroma of roasting meat and garlic.

Jake Barnes and countless Hemingway anecdotes would send us upstairs at Botín, but we choose the seclusion of the wine cave downstairs on this bustling afternoon. The food here is as true as these centuries-old brick buttresses holding up the main-floor dining room and all those formally dressed waiters—in a cave surrounded by the smell of fermented grapes and meat, a Hemingway's oasis.

We keep the order simple, Botín's darlings, *Cochinillo Asado con Patatas Asadas* (page 32) and *Sopa de Ajo* (page 35), roasted suckling pig and garlic soup. And there's always wine, "the great giver of happiness and well-being and delight."

After a spell of listening to the bricks share their stories, a portion of *cochinillo* arrives to the table. It's garnished with some buttery potatoes. The skin is crisp, and the meat is tender, barely holding on to the bone. There is nothing nuanced about this dish. Fire, salt, olive oil, perhaps a branch of thyme or rosemary thrown in for aroma. Hemingway enjoyed foods for what they were, and this was that. Botín and the eighteenth-century wood oven have endured on this very philosophy. It's primal.

Though a fork and knife make one feel civilized while digging into the roast, that ruby glass of Rioja Alta doesn't hurt. Its oaky, sharp, clean character cuts through the lush bites of pork perfectly. Hemingway, always particular about his wine, held Rioja Alta at the top; it played nicely with the robust flavors of Spanish cooking. This pure and balanced duet of meat and drink echoes Hemingway's sentiment that food isn't mere sustenance. It's culture and it's a way to connect. In this restaurant with aging walls, deep roots, and possible ghosts, this bite and this sip in this moment *is* Spain.

Then, the table gets more crowded, adding to the cultural mash. *Sopa de ajo*, garlic soup. Rich broth thickened with bread, dusted with paprika, spiked with bits of cured ham, with a poached egg to mix in. This was the aroma from the doorway. Garlic. Hemingway wrote of long braided strands of the stuff, hanging in shops, caves, outside of homes, and around the necks of revelers. Ever-present, emblematic of Spanish cooking. They say it wards off evil spirits. And that may or may not be true, but why take chances.

The soup, a few more ingredients than our roast, but still a humble dish. One that appealed to Hemingway's taste for the austere, one that warms on a brisk day. Hands wrapped on the bowl, breathing in the steam until it thins. Restorative.

Not quite full but sated for now. After the meal and last sips of wine, we walk. Hemingway would have had it no other way for a good think. It clears the head, lets one take in the city in a way that two or four wheels make impossible. This, the country Hemingway adored, with Madrid at its core, was indeed the capital of the world in his eyes. Where "the best way to get a good life is to live it," and live it they do. Narrow lanes echo with the buzz of friends gathering over a table and lead to grand plazas with more of the same. The good life on display.

We choose to wander away from the bustle. The old neighborhoods of the Latin and literary quarters, with afternoon shadows cast over cobblestone, offer the maze of medieval facades that speak to us the loudest. In these twisting alleyways live the spirits of some of Hemingway's Spanish muses armed with pens—Baroja, Cervantes, and Quevedo—who inspired his focus on the verve of everyday life. Despite the cacophony of poetry and prose from the past, it's quiet here. Just quiet enough to send our thoughts back to food, the classics of Madrid, and those buzzy lanes of cafés we left behind.

To Taberna de la Daniela for their raison d'être and what seems an indulgent next stop, *cocido madrileño*, or Madrid stew. This multicourse feast begins with thin noodles and a broth in which meats and vegetables take a long swim. These swimmers then find their own platter as the second course. Luckily, Daniela has on offer the first course à la carte for those who wish to merely get the gist of the *cocido*.

The broth arrives in its bare brilliance. Hemingway would have approved. He often sought the realness, the essence of a place, and this bowl fills that niche. Diverse elements drawn together, boiled down to something greater than the sum of its parts. That broth is much like Madrid. Vibrant, complex, vital, delightful. Along with this liquid gold and *fideo* pasta, a few garbanzos are tossed in as a garnish. A nice touch.

With appetites revived, there is one final act to round out our foray in Hemingway's Madrid. After winding our way once again through the labyrinthine streets of the historic center, we stop at a small hotel bar, Tablafina. It's the kind of place you'd miss if you weren't looking for it. It's also the kind of place that has a secret worth sharing. Hemingway would have been first in line if there were one. He'd also be pining for seafood by this point. We order their *Bocadillo de Calamares* (page 36), a fried squid sandwich.

This ironic icon of landlocked Madrid is typically served on a long roll with giant battered rings of squid and aioli. Here, the form is smaller, better for a quick bite, both in its toasty bun and crispy, tiny rounds of calamari. The sauce infused with garlic. Perfect, simple, and satisfying, all washed down with a cold beer.

With the sun out the window getting lower in the sky, the rhythm of Madrid begins to slow. The golden glow on the rooftops tells us it's near the end of day. We think about closing with something sweet. Hemingway wasn't a devotee to dessert, but perhaps a slice of *Tarta de Santiago* (page 33) would at least have meaning. The famed almond cake is named for the patron saint of Galicia in Spain's north, and it is a symbol of the religious pilgrimage that ends there. Many of Hemingway's characters, namely Santiago, the old man at sea, and perhaps Don Ernesto himself, were pilgrims in a way. Searching, like us.

As we wend our way through the streets and eventually lay our heads for a brief rest at The Palace Hotel, where the ghost of Hemingway peers beyond the Neptune fountain onto the grounds of the Prado museum, we're satisfied. With her quintessential Spanish vitality, Madrid has shown her spirit in every bite, every sip, and every step through its winding history. And this day was only the beginning.

"We lunched up-stairs at Botín's. It is one of the best restaurants in the world. We had roast young suckling pig and drank Rioja Alta."

—*The Sun Also Rises*

COCHINILLO ASADO CON PATATAS ASADAS

Roasted Suckling Pig and Potatoes

TOTAL TIME: 3 hours, 45 minutes
SERVES: 6 to 8 as an entrée

In literature, *cochinillo asado*, roast suckling pig, first appeared in *Don Quixote* by Miguel de Cervantes. Our hero and his sidekick, Sancho Panza, pass by an alfresco wedding where a dozen piglets are being prepared over an open fire, a practice deeply associated with the Castilian plateau since Roman times. In *The Sun Also Rises*, Hemingway uses the rustic dish cooked in the three-hundred-year-old fire at Sobrino de Botín as both a perfect comfort meal and, like the Man of La Mancha, a nod to simpler times.

9-to-11-pound piglet or suckling pig, cleaned and butterflied by a butcher

2 tablespoons kosher salt

1 cup dry white wine

2 sprigs fresh rosemary

2 sprigs fresh thyme

5 cloves garlic, lightly crushed

2 tablespoons lard

2 tablespoons extra-virgin olive oil

Preheat the oven to 350°F at least 30 minutes in advance. Evenly rub the piglet with the salt. Place the piglet skin-side down on a rack in a roasting pan. Pour an inch of wine or water into the bottom of the pan, assuring no contact with the piglet. Transfer the pan to the oven and roast for 90 minutes.

Remove the pan from the oven. Carefully turn the piglet over, skin-side up. Add the rosemary, thyme, and garlic to the liquid in the pan. Use a needle to prick the skin in several places to prevent bubbles from forming during the remainder of the roasting time. Evenly brush the skin side with the lard and olive oil. Replenish the liquid at the bottom of the pan to an inch in depth.

Return the pan to the oven and roast for another 45 minutes. Raise the temperature of the oven to 400°F and continue to roast for another 30 to 45 minutes, until the skin is very crispy, but not charred.

Remove the pan from the oven and transfer the roast to a rimmed platter. Carefully strain the accumulated liquids from the bottom of the pan into a serving vessel. Use a spoon to discard any fat that floats to the top. Portion the meat for diners and serve alongside roasted potatoes and the roasting *jus*.

Brett: *"How do you feel, Jake? My God! What a meal you've eaten."*
Jake: *"I feel fine. Do you want a dessert?"*
Brett: *"Lord, no."*

—*The Sun Also Rises*

TARTA DE SANTIAGO
Almond Flour Cake

TOTAL TIME: 50 minutes
SERVES: 6 to 8 as a dessert

Originally called the *tarta real*, or royal cake, the *tarta de Santiago* was for those who could afford the main ingredient, almonds. In other words, the rich. Almonds got cheaper and eventually a creative pastry chef from Santiago de Compostela in Galicia used powdered sugar and a stencil to mark the top of the cake with the cross of the town's namesake, Saint James. Over time, the cake became associated with the Camino de Santiago de Compostela, the pilgrimage that ends at the eponymous cathedral in the eponymous town.

Butter for greasing

1¼ cups sugar

5 eggs

2 teaspoons lemon zest

1 teaspoon ground cinnamon

1 tablespoon Amaretto or another almond liqueur

2 cups almond flour

Confectioners' sugar, for dusting

Chocolate sauce, for drizzling (optional)

Whipped cream, for topping (optional)

Preheat the oven to 350°F. Grease a 10-inch springform pan with butter. In a stand mixer fitted with a paddle attachment, cream the sugar and eggs until pale and smooth. Add the lemon zest, cinnamon, and liqueur and mix until incorporated. Gradually add the almond flour and continue blending until a smooth batter forms.

Transfer the batter into the greased springform pan and then into the oven. Bake for 30 to 40 minutes, until a cake tester or toothpick comes out clean. Allow the cake to cool in the pan, then transfer it to a serving platter. Dust with confectioners' sugar and slice per diner. Drizzle each slice with chocolate sauce and top with whipped cream, if using.

". . . out now from the odors of different herbs whose names he did not know that hung in bunches from the ceiling, with long ropes of garlic, away now from the copper-penny, red wine and garlic, horse sweat and man sweat dried in the clothing . . . Robert Jordan breathed deeply of the clear night air of the mountains that smelled of the pines and of the dew on the grass in the meadow by the stream."

—FOR WHOM THE BELL TOLLS

SOPA DE AJO

Garlic Soup

TOTAL TIME: 25 minutes

SERVES: 4 to 6 as an appetizer

We had the opportunity to chat with Sobrino de Botín owner and keeper of the flame, Antonio González. After sharing tales of Hemingway's frequent visits and where he (actually) sat, mixed martinis, drank, and scribbled notes during all hours, Antonio introduced us to Chef Hector Martín Aranda. They toured us through the kitchen and proudly highlighted the storied three-hundred-year-old fire in the oven. Then, as if mass had begun in the church of González, we got the sermon we didn't know we deserved on the sanctity of *sopa de ajo*. This is our adaptation of Chef Hector's nearly holy garlic soup.

¼ cup extra-virgin olive oil

10 to 12 cloves garlic, minced

4 ounces Spanish ham or *Jamón Ibérico*, diced (optional)

1 tablespoon sweet smoked paprika

6 ounces crusty bread, toasted and cubed

1 teaspoon kosher salt

½ teaspoon freshly ground black pepper

6 cups chicken stock

4 to 6 eggs

Preheat the oven to 400°F.

Add the olive oil to a 2- or 3-quart pot over medium heat. When the oil begins to shimmer, add the garlic and ham, if using, and sauté for 2 to 3 minutes, until very fragrant and the garlic is golden. Add the paprika, bread, salt, and pepper, and continue to sauté for 3 minutes, until the bread is well coated with seasoned oil.

Increase the heat to high and pour in the stock. When the liquid comes to a boil, reduce the heat to low. Stir the soup until the bread has broken down into the desired-size pieces and the broth has thickened slightly, about 4 minutes.

Evenly ladle the soup into 4 to 6 oven-safe vessels, such as ceramic ramekins. Crack an egg into the middle of each individual ramekin, place them on a baking sheet, and transfer the baking sheet to the oven. Roast for 10 minutes, or until the egg white is fully cooked and the yolk is still jiggly. Serve hot out of the oven and encourage diners to mix in the egg.

"Here there were concentrations of shrimp and bait fish and sometimes schools of squid in the deepest holes and these rose close to the surface at night where all the wandering fish fed on them."

—*The Old Man and the Sea*

BOCADILLO DE CALAMARES

Fried Squid Sandwich

TOTAL TIME: 30 minutes
SERVES: 2 as an entrée

Even before the building of the railroads in nineteenth-century Spain, Madrid made it a priority to get fresh fish and seafood from the coast to the heart of the city in time for the next meal. And since squid was cheap and plentiful, a sandwich overfilled with crispy fried rings became emblematic of a worker's lunch. Today, it remains an oddly iconic snack for an inland metropolis, but iconic it is.

GARLIC-LEMON AIOLI

1 large egg

1 tablespoon freshly squeezed lemon juice

2 cloves garlic or ½ teaspoon garlic powder

¼ teaspoon kosher salt

¾ cup vegetable oil

FRIED SQUID

8 ounces squid rings, room temperature, rinsed and patted dry

½ teaspoon kosher salt

Canola or vegetable oil, for frying

⅔ cup all-purpose flour

2 eggs

SANDWICH

2 ciabatta or other crusty sandwich rolls, halved

Black garlic aioli, as needed

1 lemon, cut into wedges

TO MAKE THE GARLIC-LEMON AIOLI: In a large mixing bowl sitting atop barely wet paper towels (keeping the bowl in place), place the egg, lemon juice, garlic, and salt. Whisk briskly while slowly drizzling in the oil until a white aioli forms to the desired consistency. Whisk in 2 tablespoons of water, 1 teaspoon at a time, as needed. Alternatively, combine all the ingredients, including the water, in a glass measuring cup and blend well using an immersion blender.

TO MAKE THE FRIED SQUID: In a mixing bowl, coat the squid rings with the salt. Pour enough oil into a skillet to about 1 inch in depth. Heat the oil to 350°F over medium heat. If you don't have a thermometer, one handy trick is to use a wooden chopstick to check the heat. As the oil heats, touch the tip of the chopstick to the bottom of the skillet at an angle. Once you see lots of bubbles forming around the entirety of the submerged chopstick, the oil is ready.

Prepare a wire rack over a baking sheet and place next to the stove.

In a mixing bowl, coat all the rings of squid with flour. Transfer the floured squid rings to a strainer and sift away any excess flour. In a separate mixing bowl, whisk the eggs. Transfer the flour-dusted squid rings into the whisked eggs and stir to ensure the rings do not clump together. Carefully drop each coated ring into the hot oil. Work in batches and do not overcrowd the pan. Fry each squid ring until golden brown, about 2 to 3 minutes in total. Remove the fried squid to the wire rack and repeat with the remaining rings.

TO BUILD THE SANDWICHES: Toast the roll halves. Smear the inside of each roll with aioli, then top the bottom halves with fried squid rings, followed by the top of the roll. Serve with lemon wedges for squeezing.

CHAPTER 2

SIMPLE, HONEST, ROBUST

As Food Should Be

"Tapas: or covers, so called since they were originally placed across the top of the glass instead of being served on small saucers as now, are the appetizers . . . which are served free with Manzanilla wine or vermouth, in cafés, bars, or bodegas."

—*DEATH IN THE AFTERNOON*

Waking from a siesta can be tough. And since somebody turned off the sun while we weren't looking, it can also be disorienting. We throw our trust at the clock on the wall rather than our mildly jet-lagged selves. Suddenly, it's night. Just to confirm, we step onto the balcony and eye Neptune watching over his fountain, now aglow. The crowds below have swelled, and the air is crisp. We're hungry and need a walk. But first, some fuel.

As Hemingway exclaimed in the voice of Jake Barnes, "It's funny what a wonderful gentility you get in the bar of a big hotel." As Jake and Lady Brett may agree, The Palace certainly fit the bill. Our barkeep is pleasantly chatty, and that helps keep us awake, though the lights are low, adding a wrinkle. The room is opulent, the patrons sharp, and the stools oddly comfortable for stools. The garrulous barkeep turns into an artist as he shakes our martinis frosty and pours.

That first sip of cold, sharp gin, despite the illusion of vermouth, cuts through our siesta haze. No nonsense, just the juice, a tap of the power switch. Now awake and aware of the need to eat, we order a plate of oysters to match the room. Chic yet dressed only with the squeeze of a lime. A luxury, to be sure, but we enjoy the occasional hit of regal amid authenticity. As Hemingway said of oysters, we "lost the empty feeling and began to be happy and to make plans."

We have the night ahead and intend to do it right. Keeping true to the mantra of what Hemingway thought of Spanish cooking—simple, honest, and robust—a tapas crawl is the plan. We imagine starting at another Hemingway favorite Madrid restaurant, and El Callejón would be the place had it not closed years ago. Poetically standing in its place is a Cuban bar. His description of the erstwhile menu is at least an inspiration: "the best vegetables, fish, meats and fruits that were in the markets and simple, wonderful cooking . . . and the wine was excellent." Marching orders, indeed.

As a *callejón* is the alleyway between the sand of a bullring and the grandstand, we choose to eat our way up Calle de la Cava Baja, another curved lane. Cava Baja has cultural depth, more so than just the bullring analogy. It follows the footprint of the ancient city wall. As city walls do, this one came down and the footprint became a road, that road became a marketplace, that marketplace was full of traders, and those traders needed to eat. End to end *tascas*, the people's bars.

Cava Baja captures Hemingway's draw to history, most certainly to food, and to the buzz that came with the throngs of people out to do what we're here to do. Eat, drink, and embrace humanity. Hemingway famously said, "Don't bother with churches, government buildings or city squares, if you want to know about a culture, spend a night in its bars." You don't linger too long in one place. Like Hemingway's cast of characters across tales, we sip, we eat, we move.

The next few hours are a parade of famous places, classic tapas, and cheery conversation with new friends. Bars that seem to speak to Hemingway directly. Taberna la Concha, a name that evokes his favorite Basque Country beach, and

happens to have a button on the bar one pushes to receive a cold glass of cava. That doesn't hurt. La Posada del Dragón, which houses remnants of that old city wall. Casa Lucas, with its rustic lack of airs that Hemingway found grounding.

Our food choices reflect Hemingway's view of Spanish cooking. In the right hands, a few humble ingredients become something greater, something profound. *Queso Manchego con Miel y Avellanas* (page 40), semi-cured cheese with hazelnuts and honey, the sharpness of the cheese meets a bitter-sweet crunch. *Chorizo al Vino* (page 43), sausage braised in garlic and red wine, a Hemingway home run of sorts. *Hongos de Temporada y Yema* (page 44), seasonal mushrooms with a runny egg yolk, a taste of the land itself. Real food, like good writing, doesn't need excess.

As we travel mere feet from bar to bar, the night alive with the voices of strangers becoming comrades over shared songs, the clink of glasses, and offering bites among tables, the city unfolds as a story being written before our eyes. Like any good story, it has to end right.

We amble toward The Palace in denial of the late hour, and like a beacon, the lighted sign atop The Ritz redirects us from a few hundred feet away. While in Paris, Hemingway would hold court at The Ritz bar, mixing drinks for fellow war correspondents, a gesture of normalcy in a French city under siege. We take a moment to honor Paris Hemingway with a sip.

Pictura Bar at The Ritz is a sight to behold. The walls are lined with portraits of contemporary Spanish celebrities dressed in the Baroque style, a nod to the Prado, which is within view. The barkeep was also in a classical style, but closer to the 1930s than the 1730s. White jacket, black bow tie, slick hair, mustache, large nickeled shaker, clearly uniformed to pour well. We order a *Papa Doble* (page 41), Hemingway's daiquiri of lime and grapefruit, with a touch of maraschino, scratch the sugar, and double the rum. The essentials.

An unwritten rule of tapas, for each drink, order one plate, though we get two and have an idea. A portion of *jamón Ibérico de bellota*, the best Spanish ham fed with acorns, and *Croquetas de Jamón* (page 47) flavored with the same. The croquette is thin and crisp on the outside, rich and creamy with meaty bits within. We cap each perfectly fried ball with an expertly sliced, translucent film of *jamón*. A tapa on a tapa. Now, that is the way to end the story.

"I kept a cold bottle of the light rosado of Campanas in the ice bag and ate bread with a slab of Manchegan cheese with it. I loved this country in all seasons and was always happy to come through the last pass and move into the harshness of La Mancha and Castille."

—*The Dangerous Summer*

QUESO MANCHEGO CON MIEL Y AVELLANAS

Manchego Cheese with Honey and Hazelnuts

TOTAL TIME: 5 to 7 minutes

SERVES: 3 to 4 as a tapa

Spain can learn from the French and the Italians when it comes to marketing their cheeses internationally. Manchego, the cheese of La Mancha, is one that broke through to other countries' radar. Still, it typically only appears on cheese boards alongside olives, hams, and peppers. In Spain, however, one finds the cheese on sandwiches, in pastry, marinated, and mixed in with other flavorful friends. This is one of the simple and best we've encountered.

3 tablespoons extra-virgin olive oil

3 tablespoons honey

8 ounces aged Manchego cheese, diced

¼ cup roasted, unsalted hazelnuts, crushed

In a medium mixing bowl, whisk together the olive oil and honey. Fold in the cheese. Serve in a separate small bowl for presentation, topped with crushed hazelnuts, and perhaps toothpicks alongside to make grabbing the bites easier.

"Nobody goes to bed in Madrid until they have killed the night. Appointments with a friend are habitually made for after midnight at the café. In no other town that I have ever lived in, except Constantinople during the period of the Allied occupation, is there less going to bed for sleeping purposes."

—*Death in the Afternoon*

PAPA DOBLE

Hemingway Daiquiri

TOTAL TIME: 5 minutes
SERVES: 2 cocktails

In Madrid, at Pictura Bar in the Mandarin Oriental Ritz, David Ferrero is that barkeep in classic style without embellishment. His dress matches his perspective on the art. We reminisce about classic cocktails, the martini, and a true daiquiri in particular. He notes that in an increasingly complex world, throw-back simplicity is refreshing, and Hemingway's spirit lingering at the bar agrees. Here is David's version of the *Papa Doble*, originally crafted for Hemingway in Cuba.

¾ ounce maraschino liqueur
1 ounce freshly squeezed lime juice
2½ ounces grapefruit juice
4 ounces white rum
2 twists orange peel

To a cocktail shaker half-filled with ice, add the maraschino, lime juice, grapefruit juice, and rum and shake until the outside of the shaker is ice-cold. Strain the daiquiris into 2 chilled glasses and garnish each with an orange peel.

CHATEAU

"Wine is one of the most civilized things in the world and one of the natural things of the world that has been brought to the greatest perfection, and it offers a greater range for enjoyment and appreciation than, possibly, any other purely sensory thing which may be purchased."

—*Death in the Afternoon*

CHORIZO AL VINO

Red Wine Chorizo

TOTAL TIME: 45 minutes
SERVES: 3 to 5 as a tapa

La Rioja is a highly productive wine-growing region in the north of Spain, but at this point, that's clear to the world. What may not be as clear is what happens to all that wine that is not shipped around the world or consumed domestically. In La Rioja, inventive chefs use what remains to create distinctly *Riojana* cuisine. One brilliant example is braising and elevating blander foods in wine. In the case of chorizo, it may be gilding the lily, but sometimes the lily doesn't mind.

2 tablespoons extra-virgin olive oil

4 cloves garlic, peeled, lightly crushed

2 links Spanish chorizo or other smoked sausage, cut into ½-inch disks

1 cup red wine

Crusty bread, for dipping (optional)

Add the olive oil and garlic to a skillet over medium heat. When the oil begins to shimmer, place the sausage slices flat along the bottom. Sear the sausages on each side for 4 to 5 minutes, until well browned. Remove the garlic from the skillet and discard. Pour in the wine, increase the heat to high and bring to a boil. Reduce the heat to low and maintain a simmer for 20 minutes.

Remove the sausages to a rimmed platter and continue to simmer the wine sauce until slightly thickened, about 5 to 6 additional minutes.

Pour the sauce over the sausage slices and serve hot with crusty bread for dipping or simply some toothpicks for grabbing.

"Each knew how the other felt and they sat there and Robert Jordan ate the stew, taking time to appreciate the mushrooms completely, and he drank the wine and they said nothing."

—*For Whom the Bell Tolls*

HONGOS DE TEMPORADA Y YEMA

Seasonal Mushrooms with Egg Yolk

TOTAL TIME: 25 minutes
SERVES: 3 to 4 as a tapa

We had the chance to speak with Carles Grau of Bar del Pla in Barcelona about the growing Slow Food movement across Spain. The focus of the trend is on natural foods and cuisine remaining as close to the earth as possible before showing up on a plate. Cultivation techniques within the natural foods' world are a lot closer to Hemingway's time than our own. He would have appreciated the pureness and the results. According to Carles, seasonal mushrooms, and this dish in particular, are emblematic of the movement. Chefs across the country have their own spin. Here is an adaptation of the dish from Bar del Pla's Chef Jordi Peris.

WHITE GARLIC SAUCE (MAKES ABOUT 1½ CUPS)

½ cup blanched almonds

3 ounces white bread (about 2 to 3 slices), crusts discarded, and torn into bite-size pieces

1 clove garlic

1 tablespoon sherry vinegar

¼ teaspoon kosher salt

¼ cup extra-virgin olive oil

MUSHROOMS

2 tablespoons extra-virgin olive oil

2 cloves garlic

12 ounces fresh wild mushrooms, brushed and stemmed

¼ teaspoon kosher salt

¼ teaspoon freshly ground black pepper

3 egg yolks

Microgreens, for garnish

Crusty bread, for serving

TO MAKE THE WHITE GARLIC SAUCE: Place all the ingredients, along with 1 cup of water, in a blender and purée until smooth. Add additional water 1 teaspoon at a time until the consistency of a creamy salad dressing is achieved. Set aside. Leftover garlic sauce can be refrigerated for up to 1 week.

TO MAKE THE MUSHROOMS AND FINISH: Add the olive oil to a skillet over medium heat. When the oil begins to shimmer, add the garlic and sauté until golden, about 3 minutes. Remove the garlic and discard. Add the mushrooms to the skillet and sauté for 5 minutes. Add the salt and pepper and continue to sauté for 5 to 9 minutes, until cooked through and beginning to brown at the edges.

Add ½ to 1 cup of the white garlic sauce to the skillet. The more sauce added, the more bread that can be dipped. Bring the mixture to a simmer over high heat. Reduce the heat to low and continue to simmer for 5 minutes.

Pour the hot mushroom mixture into individual rimmed serving dishes and top each portion with a whole egg yolk and microgreens. Invite diners to stir in the yolks immediately to create the final sauce. Serve with crusty bread.

"There was a huge cooked ham, rosy and white edged in a half-opened tin on the table beside my typewriter and a comrade would reach up, cut himself a slice of ham with his pocket knife, and go back to the crap game. I cut myself a slice of ham."

—"NIGHT BEFORE BATTLE"

CROQUETAS DE JAMÓN
Ham Croquettes

TOTAL TIME: 15 minutes, plus overnight, plus 25 minutes
SERVES: 7 to 9 as a tapa

As Americans adopted pizza as their own, with myriad permutations compared to the original from Italy, so, too, have Spaniards adopted the *croqueta*. These crispy then creamy morsels are a French innovation created to use up leftover bits of meats, cheese, and vegetables, but they've taken on a life of their own on the tapas table. Indeed, *croquetas* may well be the most universal tapa in Spain, and those adorned with *jamón*, the pepperoni pizza of them all.

BASE

¼ cup unsalted butter

¼ cup extra-virgin olive oil

2 cloves garlic, minced

1 cup all-purpose flour

4 cups whole milk, warmed

¼ teaspoon kosher salt

8 ounces *Jamón Ibérico de Bellota* or other premium Spanish ham, finely diced

CROQUETTES

1 cup all-purpose flour

1 egg

1 cup fine breadcrumbs

Vegetable or canola oil, for frying

4 ounces *Jamón Ibérico de Bellota* or other premium Spanish ham, very thinly sliced

TO MAKE THE BASE: Add the butter and olive oil to a saucepan over medium heat. As the butter melts, add the garlic and flour and sauté for 2 minutes. Slowly whisk in milk until smooth. When the mixture comes to a boil, reduce the heat to medium-low, add salt and continue to whisk for 2 minutes. Turn off the heat and vigorously stir in the diced ham.

Pour the filling into a rimmed baking dish and flatten the top with plastic wrap. Transfer to the refrigerator to cool for at least 3 hours, overnight is ideal.

TO MAKE THE CROQUETTES: Preheat the oven to 300°F. Remove the base from the refrigerator and peel away the plastic. Slice the mass into 24 equal portions and use wet hands to form balls. Set each aside on a lightly floured surface.

Using 3 shallow bowls or pie pans, set up a dredging station. First, the flour. Second, the egg with 1 tablespoon water whisked together. Third, breadcrumbs. Place a clean plate at the end of the dredging station. Lightly coat each formed croquette with flour. Then coat with egg mixture. Finally, coat with breadcrumbs and place on the plate.

Pour ½ inch of oil into a skillet and heat to 360°F. If you don't have a thermometer, you can use a wooden chopstick: When bubbles form all around the submerged portion, the oil is ready.

Prepare a wire rack over a baking sheet and place it next to the stove.

Carefully lower each coated croquette into the hot oil. Work in batches to prevent overcrowding. Occasionally turn the croquettes so they brown evenly on all sides, about 2 to 3 minutes in total. Use a slotted spoon to remove them from the oil and place them on the wire rack. Transfer the rack to the oven to keep the croquettes warm while frying the remainder.

Serve *croquetas* hot with a plate of ham slices and direct diners to place a slice atop a hot croquette before eating.

CHAPTER 3

MORNING WALK

The Park

"We can get an apartment in Madrid on that street that runs along the Parque of the Buen Retiro . . . . There are apartments there that face on the park and you can see all of the park from the windows; the iron fence, the gardens, and the gravel walks and the green of the lawns where they touch the gravel, and the trees deep with shadows and the many fountains, and now the chestnut trees will be in bloom."

—*For Whom the Bell Tolls*

Hemingway once said, "When I am working on a book or a story I write every morning as soon after first light as possible. There is no one to disturb you and it is cool or cold and you come to your work and warm as you write." We embrace the brisk as we amble through the city before she awakens in earnest. That is our work and Madrid at sunrise, our office. The analogy stops here, as churros make for a terrible typewriter. Then again, the chocolate is piping hot, and Café Chocolat is at the heart of the literary quarter. There is that.

The sight of churros and chocolate evokes dessert, but Hemingway seldom wrote of sugary treats at the end of a meal. No, this is breakfast to a Spaniard, and surprisingly unsweet. The churros are crispy and a bit salty. The sipping chocolate, dark, almost bitter and smoky. Let's say it's a wink to Hemingway's World War I injury sustained while delivering chocolate to troops on the Italian front. We dunk, then swirl the churro to get the best possible ebony coat, bite, and just like that, our late-night tapas revelry vanishes, and we finally imagine room enough for more food. But first, we stretch our legs.

Retiro Park is an escape for busy *Madrileños*, a chance to dip out of the bustle. Even as a daydream in *For Whom the Bell Tolls*, the park offers Maria and Robert Jordan, ever the idealist, a glance at what life can be had without war. The stately promenades, the botanical allure, the cheerful fountains that beckon the world-weary. For us, with no time clock to punch, no fascists to forget, and no particular bustle at this hour, Retiro is just a pleasant stroll.

We witness Madrid come to life at its pace. For Hemingway, who built volumes on the little rituals of life, Retiro was full while nearly empty. The few bundled-up rowers on the pond, the early picnic with a lover before work, the coffee cart's first puffs of steam, a pre-school game of tag, yet unburdened by the city's demands. A way to press pause among the trees and the statues worn in places rubbed by thousands we will never meet.

Perhaps it is the memory of that coffee cart or the aroma of its steam, but something about this walk makes us thirsty and strangely hungry. Too far from the cart now to make it worth moving backward. Always see something new, they say. We exit the park to the north. The Salamanca neighborhood lies across the street. It's modern, a far cry from Hemingway's twisted historic alleyways of El Centro. *Always* see something new.

While we were away, as far away as a park gate allows, the city has started to move. There's the bustle. Past the honking cars zipping to work and not too deep into Salamanca lies what those in-the-know find is the finest *Tortilla Española de Patatas* (page 50). Casa Dani gets crowded inside the La Paz Market, so we sit at its less-noticed patio just outside the market doors. We are now those in-the-know, and the patio doesn't stay uncrowded for long. Better still, more smiles to be seen as slices of

tortilla find each table. We order ours, some toast smeared with tomato, and *café con leche*.

Arriving at our table, Hemingway's ideal of simple, straightforward food in the right hands. The kind of dish a kid from the Midwest might liken to a grandmother's hug, and one that he may have whipped up for a crowd in his room at the Hotel Florida across town. A wedge from a warm disk of eggs, tender potatoes, onions, and salt. A thin layer of curd holding together a creamy center. Each bite a revelation of texture and luxury. In Spain, this work of simple genius is eaten any time. To us, eggs mean breakfast, and this was the right way to begin our day. After that appetizer of churros and chocolate, that is. The Prado must be open by now.

Bill: *"First the chicken; then the egg."*

Jake: *"Wonder what day God created the chicken?"*

Bill: *"Oh, how should we know? We should not question. Our stay on earth is not for long. Let us rejoice and believe and give thanks."*

Jake: *"Eat an egg."*

—*The Sun Also Rises*

TORTILLA ESPAÑOLA DE PATATAS
Spanish Potato Tortilla

TOTAL TIME: 50 minutes (optionally, add time to caramelize the onions)
SERVES: 4 to 6 as a tapa, 2 to 3 as an entrée

The iconic *tortilla española* de patatas offers cloudlike chunks of fried spuds and sometimes softened onions suspended in a custard of whisked eggs. Onions are the subject of fiery debate across Spain, where we have the "with-onion" crowd, *con-cebollistas*, and on the other side, the "without-onion" devotees, *sin-cebollistas*! *Sin-cebollistas* either believe in the humility of the potato and consider any interlopers to be flourish, or that onion delivers an unnecessary sweetness to the dish. When crafted properly, however, potatoes and onions can wed into a third identity entirely. Onions are certainly optional, though we lean *con-cebolla*.

1 large onion, thinly sliced (optional)

1 pound potatoes (1 to 2 large), peeled and sliced into ¼-inch-thick half-moons

4 tablespoons extra-virgin olive oil, divided

1½ teaspoons kosher salt, divided

6 large eggs

Preheat the oven to 375°F. If using, begin caramelizing the onions at the appropriate time ahead of the rest of the recipe.

In a mixing bowl, evenly toss the potato slices with 2 tablespoons of the olive oil and 1 teaspoon of salt. Evenly spread onto a baking sheet in one layer and cover with aluminum foil. Transfer the baking sheet to the oven and roast until the potatoes can easily be pierced with a knife, about 30 to 35 minutes.

Remove the potatoes from the oven and uncover. Transfer to a large mixing bowl and lightly crush the potatoes with a fork or masher. Add the eggs, the remaining ½ teaspoon of salt, and, optionally, the caramelized onions. Use a fork to whisk the mixture until even and the potatoes continue to break down slightly into the eggs.

Add the remaining 2 tablespoons of olive oil to an 8-inch nonstick skillet over medium heat. When the oil begins to shimmer, pour the egg mixture into the skillet and use a rubber spatula to move the egg mixture around occasionally as it cooks for the first 2 minutes, gently redistributing cooked curds from the bottom. Allow the bottom and sides of the tortilla to cook undisturbed for 1 minute. Swirl the pan to assure the bottom is fully cooked and not sticking.

Lightly grease the top of a plate that is wider than the skillet. Place the plate, upside down, atop the skillet. Use oven mitts if sensitive to heat. Place one hand atop the plate, another hand on the skillet handle. Carefully and in a single motion, flip the plate and skillet as if they were one object. The partially cooked tortilla should easily come away from the skillet onto the plate.

Return the skillet to low heat and slide the tortilla, wet-side down, back into the skillet using a rubber spatula. Use the spatula to tuck the tortilla back into a perfectly round shape as the bottom cooks without moving it for another 2 minutes.

Slide the tortilla onto a clean plate or serving board. Cut into wedges and serve hot or at room temperature along with *Pan con Tomate* (page 81).

NOTE ON VARIATION: *The traditional potato tortilla is a standard platform upon which one can spin innumerable dishes. Across Spain, some of the more interesting alternatives include octopus, spinach, and white beans, of course meats like chorizo and jamón, and even dark chocolate. We encourage as much creativity with a tortilla as one may put toward, say, a pasta dish, with the eggs as a reliable vehicle. We recently enjoyed a "smash burger" tortilla with onions that's worthy of a thought.*

CHAPTER 4

THE ARTS

A Dish Is Worth a Thousand Words

"Goya did not believe in costume but he did believe in blacks and in grays, in dust and in light, in high places rising from plains, in the country around Madrid, in movement, in his own cojones, in painting, in etching, and in what he had seen, felt, touched, handled, smelled, enjoyed, drunk, mounted, suffered, spewed up, lain-with, suspected, observed, loved, hated, lusted, feared, detested, admired, loathed, and destroyed."

—*Death in the Afternoon*

Hemingway called the Prado Museum's facade "as unpicturesque as an American high school building," but the inside was a different story. He enjoyed its simple arrangement, good lighting, and lack of attempt to "theatricalize" the artwork. It was one of his favorite places to be. He hardly wrote a piece about Madrid, fictional or not, in which her virtues were not lauded. Indeed, if Madrid had only the Prado, "it would be worth spending a month in every spring." We have only the afternoon.

We look to the Spanish masters, many of whom Hemingway admired. To him, Velázquez was a precise technician with efficiency and subtlety reflecting how a story ought to be told. El Greco offered an intense depiction of Spain's mystical side, for which Hemingway held fascination and skepticism. Sorolla used light and color to immortalize the dignity of the Spanish countryside. All influenced his writing and grasp of Spain, but none more than Francisco Goya.

Our time here is brief, so Goya earns our visit. His *Disasters of War* series followed closely by *The Third of May 1808* left Hemingway with brutal wartime truths; many truths show up in *For Whom the Bell Tolls*. Goya's *Black Paintings* spoke to Hemingway's search for the limits of sanity, emotion, and honesty. His thirty-three etchings in *Bullfights* were a particular favorite of Hemingway's, for obvious reasons. But we will get to that in a few pages. Be patient.

Goya's Spain knew no filters. He had the fear and the hope and the blood of it and put it all on display for us to see without turning away. We linger and look closely, losing ourselves in the layers of shadow he summoned with his brush. Goya knew where the wrinkles were and what they meant, how the soul hovered just behind the eyes. His intense, occasionally dark pieces lined up with Hemingway's own understanding of the stark and at times ugly sides of life.

There's something clean about Goya's style, despite this brutality. Straight and honest. Just as Hemingway liked his food. Like a painter, Hemingway described his meals here with such vivid sensory detail that it felt like his own canvas, creating an indelible picture of *feast* with words. Now food is in our minds. Perhaps some lunch to wash away all the gore, torture, and mania? Rightly, we venture out of the Prado with full intellect and an empty stomach. It's only fitting to sit at one of these new places, where cooks decorate plates the way an artist might a canvas, splattering sauce like Pollock or arranging greenery like Miró. But they say the food is good and Miró was a Hemingway pal.

We meet the proprietor of El MiniBar, who goes by "Nacho" and speaks of the menu as having "no rules." He is easy company, with the kind of bearded face you can trust. A face that is the subject of many satirical paintings on the walls surrounding us. Not quite the Prado. Nacho suggests a few dishes. But first, a

refreshing apéritif of *Tinto de Verano* (page 56), or red wine of summer. This glass challenges Hemingway's basic pour of Rioja with lemon soda and a bit of vermouth. It's the drinker's job to stir it all together as it arrives to the table in three colored layers. Fun, but perhaps a sign of arty things to come.

They bring the first dish, *Tapa Bretón* (page 54), a flat square of melted goat's cheese, crisp at the edges, drizzled with tomato jam that smells of cinnamon, cilantro oil, and sweet balsamic vinegar. Clearly the ghost of Picasso followed us from the Prado. And here he is on a plate. Pablo Picasso was a friend to Hemingway and their kinship went beyond the circle of the arts. Both part of a generation some call lost, disillusioned by the Great War

and both fans of the bullfight. Hemingway was critical of Picasso's abstract style, removed from the real, though he admired his tirelessness and grit as a creator. Same for the chef who made this dish. The cheese is delicious.

The next dish arrives, *Tomates Aliñados* (page 57), appearing like a fountain, but one of those fountains conceived by a sculptor and with the water turned off for the season. More a statue made of seasoned tomatoes, many varieties, each cut into building blocks reaching for the ceiling, all dressed with a pleasant vinaigrette. In sculpture, unlike painting, Hemingway did enjoy abstraction. Italian Constantin Brancusi crafted some of his favorite pieces, ironically reminiscent of Picasso's cubist work. That third-dimension changes things, it seems. The tomatoes are bright and taste of the sun, the height a bit unnecessary.

The final plate is duck, perhaps the most grounded dish, and Hemingway's game bird of choice. Goya himself may have been proud of this presentation, as the leg bone is clear and not obscured, not made to look like a tree limb or a lollipop stick. It is bone. Beneath a lacquer of prune and port, the confit leg of duck is true, tender as it should be, luscious even, and the glaze would be hard-pressed to make any improvement to it . . . only it does. What an ending.

After the meal, we walk a bit slower, as if we, too, were glazed with prune and port. It gives us time to wrap our heads around lunch. This could be a great matter of discourse, so we head to Café Gijón. In its heyday, it would have been the place to resolve this food-as-art debate. Today, gone are the intellectuals, the bohemians, the starving artists, the scribes, and other communists raring to opine. Still, there are the wood-paneled walls to offer their embrace. And a damn fine *carajillo*, a cup of joe blessed by brandy. We sit back, grateful to feel the day come into focus again, clear and simple. It's a good drink in a place we know. And that is enough.

". . . she cut him a slice, reaching up to unhook the big cheese that hung in a net from the ceiling, drawing a knife across the open end and handing him the heavy slice. He stood, eating it. It was just a little too goaty to be enjoyable."

—*For Whom the Bell Tolls*

TAPA BRETÓN
Roasted Goat Cheese

TOTAL TIME: 35 minutes
SERVES: 3 to 4 as a tapa

Ignacio "Nacho" Busto is a restaurateur for the ages and adores his guests. We were fortunate to find him doing rounds of the petite dining room of El MiniBar. He was more than pleased to curate our meal. A highlight and constant on the ever-evolving menu is the *Tapa Bretón*, named for his executive chef, José Bretón. The dish has garnered awards within Madrid's highly competitive tapas scene and exemplifies Nacho's "no rules" philosophy. Chef José's recipe is adapted below for the home kitchen.

TOMATO-CINNAMON *MERMELADA*
(MAKES ABOUT 1 CUP)

One 8-ounce can tomato purée

1 tablespoon sugar

1 stick cinnamon

CILANTRO OIL
(MAKES ABOUT 1½ CUPS)

1 cup canola or vegetable oil

¾ cup coarsely chopped cilantro

1 dash kosher salt

1 dash freshly ground black pepper

FINISH

1 tablespoon extra-virgin olive oil

8 ounces aged goat Gouda cheese, shredded

1 tablespoon balsamic vinegar

Crusty bread, for serving

Preheat the oven to 350°F.

TO MAKE THE TOMATO-CINNAMON *MERMELADA*: Add the tomato purée, sugar, and cinnamon to a small pot over medium-high heat and stir. When the tomato begins to bubble, reduce the heat to low, cover the pot, and allow the mixture to simmer for 10 minutes. Remove the cover and continue to simmer for 10 to 15 minutes, until slightly thickened. While the *mermelada* simmers, make the cilantro oil and roast the cheese. Extra *mermelada* can be refrigerated for up to 4 days.

TO MAKE THE CILANTRO OIL: Blend all the ingredients in a food processor or blender. Extra cilantro oil can be refrigerated for up to 4 days.

TO FINISH: Lightly grease a small, rimmed baking dish or baking sheet with the olive oil. Distribute an even layer of shredded cheese and transfer to the oven. Roast the cheese for 10 to 15 minutes, until the cheese is completely melted and begins to caramelize at the edges. Remove the cheese from the oven, and artfully drizzle it with desired amount of *mermelada*, cilantro oil, and balsamic vinegar. Serve hot in the baking vessel along with crusty bread.

"In it stand the sword handlers with their jugs of water, sponges, piles of folded muletas and heavy leather sword cases, the bull ring servants, the vendors of cold beer and gaseosas, of iced fruits in nets that float in galvanized buckets full of ice and water, of pastries in flat baskets, of salted almonds, and of peanuts."

—*DEATH IN THE AFTERNOON*

TINTO DE VERANO
Red Wine Spritzer

TOTAL TIME: 5 minutes
SERVES: 6 as an apéritif

Across central Spain, *Sangría* (page 110) had been the go-to way to cool off in hotter seasons using what folks were already going to drink by default: wine. In the 1960s, enterprising chefs decided that adding fruit and ice to wine wasn't enough and mixing in citrusy soda was even better to beat the heat. It stuck, and *Tinto de Verano*, or red wine of summer, was born.

3 cups ice cubes

3 cups lemon-flavored soda

One 750-milliter-bottle fruity red wine

12 tablespoons sweet vermouth

1 lemon, sliced

Half fill 6 standard wine glasses with ice cubes. Pour ½ cup of lemon soda into each. In the first glass, rest a spoon, dome-side facing up, at the edge of the ice. Slowly pour ½ cup of wine down the inside of the glass, followed by 2 tablespoons of vermouth. Each of the wines should create layers above the soda if poured carefully. Repeat with the remaining glasses. Garnish with a lemon slice and serve.

"I know no modern sculpture, except Brancusi's, that is in any way the equal of the sculpture of modern bullfighting."

—*Death in the Afternoon*

TOMATES ALIÑADOS

Dressed Tomatoes

TOTAL TIME: 20 minutes
SERVES: 3 to 4 as a tapa

In Spain it is rare to see a slice of tomato used on its own or, say, on a sandwich. The fruit is always taken a step further. Grated for *Pan con Tomate* (page 81), enveloped into *sofrito* for a paella, blended for gazpacho, etc. *Tomates aliñados,* or dressed tomatoes, offers a way to showcase the essence of the fruit itself, and presenting different tomato varieties adds to the intrigue of the dish.

2 cloves garlic, minced

2 tablespoons minced parsley

2 tablespoons extra-virgin olive oil

1 tablespoon sherry vinegar

1 to 1½ pounds tomatoes, varying in color and size

½ teaspoon kosher salt

1 tablespoon aged balsamic vinegar

In a small bowl, whisk together the garlic, parsley, olive oil, and vinegar. Set aside for at least 10 minutes.

Cut the tomatoes into decorative shapes or slices good for stacking. Lay the pieces on a baking sheet or cutting board and salt evenly.

On a serving platter, build a structure of tomatoes and get creative. It is advisable to lay a wider foundation and stack smaller layers as you go up. Drizzle the final tomato sculpture evenly with the reserved vinaigrette and aged balsamic. Serve cold or at room temperature.

"We ate him later, stuffed and roasted; and many other dishes, with the wine of that year and the year before and the great year four years before that and other years that I lost track of while the long arms of a mechanical fly chaser that wound by clockwork went round and round and we talked French. We all knew Spanish better."

—*DEATH IN THE AFTERNOON*

CONFIT DE PATO GLASEADO
Glazed Duck Confit

TOTAL TIME: Overnight, plus 4 hours, 15 minutes
SERVES: 6 to 8 as a tapa or an appetizer, 4 as an entrée

Like anywhere in the world where game birds get their time in the kitchen, Spain has a long history with duck. Over time, it's become associated with peasant dishes, since ducks were easy to raise, paired well with rice, and stood up to long cooking times in stews. This duck leg confit preparation leans French, but the glaze is very Spanish, and it's not what you would call a humble dish.

DUCK

4 whole duck legs (2½ to 3 pounds total)

1 tablespoon kosher salt

½ tablespoon freshly ground black pepper

¼ cup extra-virgin olive oil

8 cloves garlic, lightly crushed

2 shallots, coarsely chopped

GLAZE

2 cups beef stock

1 cup unsweetened prune juice

½ cup ruby port

½ teaspoon kosher salt

TO MAKE THE DUCK: Use the tip of a paring knife to prick the skin and pockets of fat on the duck legs. Do not pierce the meat. Season with salt and pepper, place in a sealed container, and refrigerate at least overnight, up to 24 hours.

Preheat the oven to 225°F.

Use a pastry brush to remove any excess salt and pepper from the duck. Place the duck legs skin-side down in a Dutch oven, along with the olive oil, garlic, and shallots. Cover the pot, transfer it to the oven, and roast for 2 hours. Remove the pot from the oven and uncover. Using a thin spatula to ensure the skin is not sticking, flip the duck legs over. Re-cover the pot and transfer it to the oven for an additional 2 hours.

TO MAKE THE GLAZE: When the duck is about 45 minutes from coming out of the oven, prepare the glaze. Add the stock, prune juice, port, and salt to a pot over medium-high heat. When the mixture comes to a boil, reduce the heat to medium and simmer for 30 to 40 minutes, until it is thickened enough to coat the back of a spoon.

TO FINISH THE DUCK: Remove the duck from the oven and transfer the legs to a baking sheet, skin-side up. Discard the garlic and shallots.

Preheat the oven to 500°F.

When the oven is at temperature, transfer the baking sheet into the oven and roast the duck for 10 to 15 minutes, until the skin has crisped. Remove the baking sheet from the oven, transfer the duck legs to a serving platter, and evenly pour over the glaze. Serve hot.

CHAPTER 5

THE BULL

Aficionado Hemingway

"There is another reason for seeing your first and last bullfight in Madrid, for the spring fights there are not during the feria season and the bullfighters are at their best."

—*Death in the Afternoon*

The brandied coffee tasted right, strong and sharp. It cleared away the pretensions, that false air that can come when plates are dressed too fine. Still, we needed that grounding feeling. The kind that comes from visiting an old friend. Hemingway's colossal chum, Las Ventas, Madrid's bullring. The arena lay silent, emptied of man and beast alike, the sand vaguely stained with centuries of old blood. There are no fights today. Just as well. Barbaric, some would say. And past its time.

Hemingway wrote in *The Sun Also Rises*, "'*Aficion*' means passion. An aficionado is one who is passionate about the bullfights." And he should know. His deep love and knowledge of the *corrida*, the bullfight, is the stuff of legend. He wrote that "Bullfighting is the only art in which the artist is in danger of death." To him, this ritualistic sport was indeed an art, a dance, a science, as mythological as it was tragic, the very soul of Spain. If one were to witness the best of all of the above, it would be in Hemingway's Madrid. This was the Broadway of blood sport.

Leftover daylight began to fade, and the ghosts felt thick, burdening. A pressure that may be relieved by saluting the sacrifices made here. We leave behind Spain's old sport for Madrid's old streets, seeking the right place to honor the bull. Matadors, if the fight was excellent, took the bull's tail as a prize, but once the ring was cleared, that tail turned to stew. *Rabo de Toro* (page 62), beef and red wine, thick and rich. Hemingway had his spots for it, Casa Alberto among them. A place with walls lined in *corrida* history, though none showed his face.

Our gaze breaks from the walls to review the bar and tables of pleased diners, unsurprisingly, each one enjoying a plate of this symbolic stew with the required red wine. Miguel de Cervantes once lived upstairs from here and wrote about windmills and impossible dreams. *Don Quixote* was an inspiration to Hemingway as an "inexhaustible study of human frailties." Perhaps this literary quest of courage, of the human spirit, and of flawed heroism informed his affection for bullfighting. But this is about the food.

We make our way to the bone, and the meat falls away with little effort from the fork. The ruby bottle of Valdepeñas matches well with the sauce. We eat knowing the bull's sacrifice, each bite a succulent act of reverence. A crusty loaf soaks up what's left. "With bread, all sorrows are less," said Sancho Panza, and we're happy.

This is not a night to fill our table with dishes. We choose instead to walk the evening away, see more of Hemingway's watering holes and find other expressions of beef. Honor is hard work. For all the moral cloud, Spain's bullrings are good at giving the bull's bravery final meaning, as they sell the meat nose to rump. That's a lot of beef. We march on to do our part.

We give our guts a break after starting with the oxtail and walk along Hemingway's Gran Vía. We begin at Callao Plaza and the ghost of his Hotel Florida home. It was ultimately demolished by planning, not Franco's bombs, though he tried, and today there's a department store. Onto the Telefónica building, with its enduring Art Deco facade, the same one Hemingway saw at every risky approach to transmit his wartime reports.

Next, a visit to Bar Chicote, Museo Chicote, as it's known today. This was Hemingway's escape with fellow

journalists during the Spanish Civil War and the first American-style pub in Spain. With a chic retro design and New York accent, Chicote's was a refuge amid the bombs. In the play *The Fifth Column*, the bar served many roles, notably as a safe haven for Philip Rawlings after visiting his butcher ahead of an air raid. Fitting for our afternoon. We have his preferred gin and tonic before moving on to our next course of beef.

Back in the literary quarter, we duck into another Hemingway haunt, Cervecería Alemana, "a good place to drink beer and coffee." His enshrined table by the window is surveilled by his photo on the wall, but we enjoy the terrace at twilight on Santa Ana Square. More people to watch and more life to feel along with a cold pilsner. We try the limited beef *salchichón*, thinly sliced coins of dried sausage, bull salami, say. Even the tougher cuts of the bull find their calling. On the square, a busker dances for happy drinkers as the *salchichón* fills our soul. Onward.

When Hemingway wasn't dodging 1930s air raids with fellow reporters, he was gathering stories from the Republican front, and La Venencia had the goods. This sherry bar a short walk away was an anti-Fascist stronghold, and passing through its doors is stepping into history. The wooden bar worn where thousands of elbows leaned and thousands of nubs of chalk tallied up drinkers' tabs before being wiped away from the record, the corded telephone mounted on the wall, the walls themselves that would whisper if they could talk.

Worth a visit for a nightcap of sherry, a dry *fino*, and maybe another bite of beef, La Venencia had some wartime rules that are still in place today. No photographs and no touching the sherry glass except by the stem. To bend the rules, one may be called out as a Francoist spy and dealt with swiftly. We're careful. We keep our phones pocketed and lift our crisp *fino* as close to the base as possible; a salty plate of *cecina*, the bovine cousin of *jamón*, pairs nicely. In this quiet place, Hemingway looms loudly.

"Rabo: tail of bull."

—*Death in the Afternoon*, Glossary

RABO DE TORO
Braised Oxtail

TOTAL TIME: 4 hours, 20 minutes
SERVES: 3 to 5 as a tapa, 2 to 3 as an entrée

Estofado de rabo de toro, or oxtail stew, grew out of Roman culinary influences on the Iberian Peninsula, like much of today's Spanish cuisine. The dish is now common across Spain and is closely associated with bullfighting, as, historically, a common "prize" to a matador for a good kill was the tail of the fallen.

2 to 3 pounds oxtails, whole

1 teaspoon freshly ground black pepper

2 teaspoons kosher salt, divided

3 tablespoons extra-virgin olive oil

1 large onion, diced

1 carrot, diced

1 large tomato, halved, stemmed, grated, and skin discarded

4 cloves garlic, minced

1 tablespoon smoked paprika

⅓ cup all-purpose flour

2 cups dry red wine

3 cups beef stock

2 tablespoons fresh parsley, coarsely chopped

Crusty bread, for serving

Preheat the oven to 275°F.

Season the oxtails using the black pepper and 1 teaspoon of the salt.

Add the olive oil to a Dutch oven or other oven-safe pot over medium-high heat. When the oil begins to shimmer, add the oxtails, in batches, if necessary. Sear the oxtails until well browned, 5 to 7 minutes in total. Using a slotted spoon, remove the beef to a plate.

Add the onion and carrot and sauté until the onion is translucent, 8 to 10 minutes. Add the tomato, garlic, paprika, and the remaining 1 teaspoon of salt and continue to sauté for an additional 2 minutes. Stir in the flour and continue to sauté for 3 minutes.

Stir in the wine and stock, increase the heat to high, and bring to a boil. Turn off the heat. Cover and transfer the pot to the oven and braise for 4 hours.

Remove the pot from the oven and carefully remove the cover. Use tongs or a slotted spoon to remove the oxtails from the sauce to a serving platter. Use an immersion blender or countertop blender to purée the sauce and pour atop the oxtails on the platter.

Garnish with parsley and serve the *rabo de toro* with crusty bread.

Part II
SEVILLA

CHAPTER 6

COMFORTLESS GRANDEUR

A City of Mixed Feelings

"We got away for Sevilla in squally weather a little after noon next day and signed in at the old Hotel Alfonso XIII with its comfortless grandeur and went to the Casa Luis to eat on the way to the bullfight. It was a good meal and a very bad bullfight."

—*THE DANGEROUS SUMMER*

The hills beyond Toledo and the Sierra Morena were a blur of tan and blue and the descent into the Guadalquivir Valley brought Sevilla into focus. We head straight to Hemingway's Sevilla lodgings, the Alfonso XIII hotel. The grand lobby, with tiled buttresses, marble and elegance, the echoes of high society's murmur lingering in the air. Hemingway called this "comfortless grandeur," dripping with gold and crystal. But Hemingway in his time held all this polish like a facade for something less welcoming, as if all the opulence helped hide this city's secrets.

Sevilla was never the city of Hemingway's heart. He respected its spirit and traditions but found the bullfighting here stained, not for the blood spilled, but for the politics that seeped into the ring. His call of corruption in Sevilla's bull business earned him little favor. The usual fanfare turned cold, the bullring itself lacked warmth, VIP treatment suddenly unavailable. In cities like Madrid or Pamplona, he'd be honored, a part of the inner fabric of bullfighting. But here in Sevilla, he was on the margin, his celebrity dimmed by money and power.

Despite it all, there was still the food. Hemingway found Sevilla's cuisine prepared with reverence for flavor, for heritage, for the simple joy of eating. We lunch at San Fernando, a restaurant amid the archways of the hotel. No matter his original reasons for lodging here, perhaps the lack of phones in the rooms keeping the Spanish press at bay, or maybe the picturesque pool in which Hemingway loved the solace of a good swim, we hear the restaurant is top-notch.

We're seated along the colonnade. The table is set with sharp silver and empty glasses catching the light. Marble columns rise around us, solid and still, as if they've stood for centuries watching diners come and go. The server in his freshly pressed shirt and vest greets us warmly, pours our glasses of Ribera del Duero Reserva. He delivers without an errant drop then moves crisp napkins from the table to our laps and sets chargers anticipating beautiful plates. Hemingway may have conceded the precision was unnerving.

The cold *Gazpacho* (page 67) arrives first, a favorite of Hemingway's and a signature dish of his fourth wife, Mary, while entertaining in Cuba. A perfect chill on the tongue smooth and rich with the essence of ripe tomatoes, cool cucumbers, and peppers. This is Sevilla in a bowl—vibrant, direct, unapologetically rooted in its own earth. Hemingway may have tasted it like an antidote to the city shutting him out, a bite of something enduring in a place that seemed to thrive on its own terms.

Next come the *Alcachofas Parrilladas* (page 69), grilled artichokes—Spain in the shape of spiny blossoms. Grilled until the outer leaves begin to curl, each bite a nutty pleasure with an overture of olive oil, garlic, and ham. Hemingway had a respect for Spain's simple dishes, and this one gets special reverence for its indigeneity. Spanish cooks handle their vegetables with pride, and this dish tells us that in Sevilla, tradition holds as firm at the stove as it *should* in the bullring. Then the pork *presa*, cut from the shoulder, marbled, and simply seared just right over the wood fire. The original pig may not have been domesticated on this peninsula, but it's honored as if it were. Hams, sausages, and every porcine muscle worth the heat are as much a part of this land as El Cid or Easter. A last pour of wine, a petite French cake, and an espresso close the meal. A reminder that Sevilla's gifts go beyond ringside seats. It's a fine indulgence. Time to swim.

"It came in a large bowl . . . with the slices of crisp cucumber, tomato, garlic bread, green and red peppers, and the coarsely peppered liquid that tasted lightly of oil and vinegar. 'It's a salad soup,' Catherine said. 'It's delicious.'"

—*The Garden of Eden*

GAZPACHO
Chilled Vegetable Soup

TOTAL TIME: 1 hour, 15 minutes
SERVES: 4 to 6 as a tapa or an appetizer

During our visit, Teresa García from the Alfonso XIII was more than hospitable and excited to highlight the hotel's 1950s history with Mary and Ernest Hemingway. She and Chef Felipe Arango designed a special "Hemingway Luncheon" and a tour of the equally Moorish and Castilian palace-turned-resort. We received the Sevillian VIP treatment that Don Ernesto so craved, which was both grand and comforting. Below are adaptations of Chef Felipe's excellent gazpacho and grilled artichokes.

4 large ripe tomatoes, cored and ¾ coarsely chopped, ¼ diced

1 small cucumber, peeled, seeded, and ¾ coarsely chopped, ¼ diced

1 small red onion, ¾ coarsely chopped, ¼ diced

1 red or yellow bell pepper, seeded and coarsely chopped

3 cloves garlic, crushed

½ teaspoon kosher salt

¼ teaspoon freshly ground black pepper

2 tablespoons sherry vinegar

1 cup extra-virgin olive oil

8 ounces (about ½ loaf) sourdough bread, crusts removed, diced, and toasted

4 ounces Spanish ham or *Jamón Ibérico*, diced (optional)

Set aside the portion of diced tomato, cucumber, and red onion for garnish. To a blender, add the remaining tomato, cucumber, onion, bell pepper, garlic, salt, and pepper. Purée for 2 to 3 minutes, until smooth. Continue to blend and add the vinegar, then slowly drizzle in the olive oil. Adjust the salt and black pepper to taste. Pass the resulting gazpacho through a fine-mesh strainer into a container. Cover and refrigerate for at least 1 hour.

Remove the gazpacho from the refrigerator. To serve, portion the soup into bowls and garnish with the reserved diced tomato, cucumber, onion, toasted bread cubes, and diced ham, if using. Alternatively, serve as a tapa in small glasses.

"'It happened all right.' David handed her the jar with the cut up artichoke heart and the dressing and found the second bottle of Tavel. It was still cool. He took a long drink of the wine. 'We've been burned out,' he said. 'Crazy woman burned out the Bournes.'"

—*The Garden of Eden*

ALCACHOFAS PARRILLADAS

Grilled Artichokes

TOTAL TIME: 45 minutes
SERVES: 2 to 4 as a tapa or an appetizer

Originally North African and eastern Mediterranean, the artichoke came to Spain with the Moors in the ninth century. In a strange twist, the Romans, notorious for artichoke reliance, were introduced to the plant *after* the Spanish, unlike most food traditions that stemmed from the Roman empire across the region.

3 artichokes, trimmed, halved, thistle and chokes removed

1 cup extra-virgin olive oil, divided

1 lemon, halved

1 teaspoon kosher salt

1 teaspoon whole black peppercorns

2 cloves garlic, thinly sliced

½ teaspoon red pepper flakes

Microgreens, for garnish

2 ounces Spanish ham or *Jamón Ibérico*, diced (optional)

To a large pot over high heat, add the artichoke halves, 6 cups of water to cover, ½ cup of the olive oil, the lemon halves, squeezed, salt, and the peppercorns and bring the mixture to a boil. Place an inverted plate atop the artichokes to keep them submerged. Reduce the heat to low, cover, and simmer for 12 to 15 minutes, until a knife slides easily into the leaves. Drain the artichokes and allow them to cool.

Add the remaining ½ cup of olive oil to a skillet over medium heat. When the oil begins to shimmer, add the garlic and pepper flakes, and sauté for 1 to 2 minutes, until the garlic begins to brown. Remove from the heat and set aside.

Prepare the grill for medium-high heat, 380°F to 450°F. Place the artichokes, cut-side down, on the grill and cook for 4 to 6 minutes undisturbed, until lightly charred. Flip the artichokes and cook for an additional 4 to 6 minutes, until the outsides have browned.

Transfer the artichokes from the grill to a plate. Drizzle with the seasoned oil, garlic, and pepper flakes and garnish with microgreens and, optionally, diced ham and additional salt.

CHAPTER 7

CAMARADERIE

Tapas in Good Company

Robert: *"Don't call me Don Roberto."*

Pilar: *"It is a joke. Here we say Don Pablo for a joke. As we say the Señorita Maria for a joke."*

Robert: *"I don't joke that way. Camarada to me is what all should be called with seriousness in this war. In the joking commences a rottenness."*

—*For Whom the Bell Tolls*

Whether on the Irati River in the Pyrenees, at La Concha beach in San Sebastián, or in the pool at Bill Davis's place outside of Málaga, Hemingway took a swim to recharge. The pool at the Alfonso was restorative, and in Hemingway's day a luxury. The cool water was an escape from the even cooler reception outside these walls. Looking upward from the chaise a row of palm trees kisses the blue sky and of nothing particularly Sevillano. This could be anywhere.

A waiter drops an apple into the pool. A wife and husband swim as if racing to see who can rescue it first. A teacher casually chats with an accountant as a young family splashes and laughs. People make this place, and we make them our people, our comrades for the afternoon. A social swim to pass the hours. We dry up and head out to find more camaraderie over some tapas. Do what Hemingway did given his war with the city's powerful and cross the river into Barrio de Triana, away from the heavy air of moneyed pride to reconnect with the salt of the earth.

Triana is the birthplace of flamenco, a home for artisans, tradespeople, and seafaring types. And bullfighters. One true thing about the *corrida* in Sevilla that Hemingway refused to defame was the matador class. He called them the best in Spain, and the locals here have a near-eligious feeling about them. In *The Dangerous Summer*, Hemingway made a beeline over the bridge from the Alfonso to the storied Triana bar now known as Casa Cuesta, and so we walk.

Here, the sun slips low, throwing long shadows over the terrace. We head inside toward the hum of locals. Hemingway wrote about this place with its good food, though he called it Casa Luis, a slip of memory perhaps for what was known as Casa Ruiz. It's a place of the people, a joint where the glasses are etched with history and the plates are honest. The air smells of peppers and brine and the dignity of knowing that this is where tapas began.

We sit at a table with an inescapable view of the television showing bullfights. The screen is hung like a painting of some saint or another and patrons' eyes are fixed in piety. The ceiling is vaulted like a cathedral, yet it only takes a few *Trianeros* to fill the heights with charm.

The televised fight was a replay from yesterday's *corrida*, so everyone is willing to divert their gaze and chat. A man at the next table notices our curiosity and raises his glass of vermouth. We raise a beer, the first of many. He talks of the *toros*, not the dirty business, not the backdoor deals or the influence of money that Hemingway despised, but the risk, the blood, the life and death that makes the *corrida* more than spectacle. Don Ernesto would have nodded, recognizing a fellow aficionado. We nod cynically, but enjoy the passion of our new comrade.

We order what they're having. There's no cause to be original when these guys know how to live. First, a dish of *Papas Aliñadas* (page 72), humble potatoes kissed with sherry vinegar and olive oil reminds us of the earth, only

brighter. Bites are firm to the tooth then suddenly creamy, the dressing tangy and bracing. There's the sea, too. Spanish chefs would add excellent canned tuna to every dish if they could get away with it. And here that's fine.

Our new amigos also enjoy a mound of crispy golden eggplant drizzled with dark molasses, *Berenjenas con Miel de Caña* (page 74) they call it, and we follow suit. Levantine-style frying, Chinese eggplant, and Indian Molasses, all a gift to Spain from the Moors. Still, the experience is decidedly Spanish.

The tapas are good, and the beers are cold, which keep us chatty with our compatriots, but it's time we move on. We could stay on the Triana side of the Guadalquivir or venture back into the center, with its siege of tourists and ghosts of Hemingway's tussle with Sevilla politics. We choose the latter. "An intelligent man is sometimes forced to be drunk to spend time with his fools," Hemingway quipped, and we've had the required beer.

We cross the street from Casa Cuesta and duck through the Callejón de la Inquisición, the fifteenth-century alleyway where those unwilling to submit to the Catholic crown took their final steps of freedom. From there, it was a fiery death or prison at the alley's end. Suddenly, a siege of tourists doesn't seem that bad.

We take the nearest bridge and ceremonially walk past La Maestranza bullring, epicenter of the bout between Hemingway and the bullfighting cartels. We wind our way into the maze of streets around the Giralda, the tallest tower on the biggest cathedral in Spain, along with throngs of tapas seekers and fellow drinkers. More comrades. Strolling guitar players provide music to the night along with the clinking of glasses, a buzz of the convivial, and hoof-falls of the occasional horse-drawn carriage.

According to the tapas night norms, we stop for a quick bite and a sip at a few bars that attract. Cervecería Giralda is our first and the closest to the cathedral that was once a mosque. The bar sits atop an ancient Moorish bathhouse, with its arched ceilings and faint echoes of Arabic. We order *Espinacas con Garbanzos* (page 77), spinach and chickpeas, a most Moorish of Spanish dishes. The spinach is soft and fragrant with cumin, paprika, and garlic, the chickpeas firm and hearty.

Onward to Bodega Santa Cruz, a no-nonsense Hemingway go-to known here as Las Columnas, where the crowd spills onto the plaza among the eponymous columns. We battle the mob to the bar, even clearing a path for fellow battlers looking to place an order. The camaraderie is repaid in toasts on our push back out to the plaza. We manage to get a plate of *Solomillo al Whiskey* (page 75), a fillet so tender it nearly gives itself to the fork, bathed in a sauce made sharp with scotch. A favorite tipple for Hemingway, but not in a crowd like this.

We also escaped from the rabble with *ensaladilla rusa*, Russian salad. An odd name for a mayonnaise, pea, and potato concoction created by a French chef that's taken on Spanish characteristics and, of course, canned tuna. As Hemingway before us, we prefer simpler dishes and the *papas aliñadas* from Casa Cuesta already filled the potato salad niche. Like Robert Jordan in *For Whom the Bell Tolls*, perhaps we've grown wary of Russian interference in our Spanish struggle. This brings a laugh among the new comrades.

It is much easier to leave the Columns than it was to enter, and we look to unwind with a final beer and an excellent tapa. Our last stop is Patanchón, a place Hemingway never knew but would have claimed as his own, with its polished wood, bustling terrace, and lack of pretension. The aroma from our perch on the plaza foretold of fried meat and pleasure. We order *Flamenquín* (page 78), a crisp roulade of chicken instead of pork, *jamón*, and cheese. The sauce is tomato sweetened with a caramel mystery, but the barkeep refuses to give up the chef's secrets. We have our ideas.

We finish the plate, wipe up the last wisps of the sauce with the French fries, and dutifully drop our stained and crumpled napkins to the floor. An aptly timed flamenco dancer spins on the plaza, her feet striking the percussion of the city, her dress whirling like a bejeweled sail. Hemingway wrote of Spain as a place of people, food, rhythm, and grace, and would have felt it all here. A final sip of beer, a final flamenco bow, and we call it a night.

Maria: "She told me she was once as slender as I but that in those days women did not take exercise. She told me what exercises I should take and that I must not eat too much. She told me which things not to eat. But I have forgotten and must ask her again."

Robert: "Potatoes."

—FOR WHOM THE BELL TOLLS

PAPAS ALIÑADAS

Potato Salad

TOTAL TIME: 25 minutes
SERVES: 3 to 5 as a tapa or an appetizer

At Casa Cuesta, amid the conversations of bulls, we were able to enjoy the exuberant hospitality of our server, Pedro Antonio Santos Perez. He had been at the restaurant long enough to have heard tales of Hemingway's visits in the 1950s. When asked about the recipes the chef used and the stalwart dishes of Hemingway's era, Pedro became visibly excited and invited Chef Francisco Moreno into our chat. The *Papas Aliñadas* was and is still a favorite, and here is our version of Chef Francisco's simple masterpiece.

2 pounds Yukon Gold potatoes, peeled and cut into 1-inch chunks

2 tablespoons plus ½ teaspoon kosher salt, divided

2 tablespoons minced parsley, plus more for garnish

¼ cup sherry vinegar

5 tablespoons extra-virgin olive oil, divided

5 ounces canned tuna in oil, drained

2 hard-boiled eggs, peeled and diced

Place the potatoes and 2 tablespoons of salt in a pot and cover the potatoes with cold water. Set the pot over high heat and bring to a boil. When the water boils, reduce the heat to medium to maintain a simmer, for 7 to 9 minutes, stirring occasionally until a piece of potato is easily pierced with a knife. Strain the potatoes in a colander, rinse with cold water, and drain completely.

Transfer the potatoes to a large mixing bowl and crush them lightly with a masher or fork. Evenly fold in the parsley, sherry, 4 tablespoons of olive oil, and the remaining ½ teaspoon of salt. Mold the salad onto 1 or 2 plates, top with large tuna flakes, cooked egg, and additional parsley. Drizzle with the remaining tablespoon of olive oil and serve.

"We came down out of the mountains and the hills past the steep, wildly confused, high-walled old gray Iberian town of Sagunto with its Roman and Moorish hodgepodge of conqueror-imposed buildings and its lovely medieval town."

—*The Dangerous Summer*

BERENJENAS CON MIEL DE CAÑA
Fried Eggplant with Molasses

TOTAL TIME: 1 hour, 20 minutes
SERVES: 6 to 8 as a tapa

Fruits in the nightshade family—eggplants, tomatoes, peppers, even potatoes—were generally thought to be unhealthy and some even toxic among Medieval Europeans. Arab traders and Jewish settlers in Spain, however, did not have such concerns. Eggplants, in particular, were a staple among Muslim and Sephardic communities on the Iberian Peninsula, and, along with molasses, made this a star dish.

- 1 globe eggplant, skin-on, cut into ½-inch batons
- ½ cup buttermilk
- ½ teaspoon kosher salt
- 1 cup all-purpose flour
- Vegetable oil, for frying
- 2 tablespoons molasses

Place the eggplant slices across the bottom of a rimmed baking sheet or baking dish in no more than two layers. Pour buttermilk and salt over the top and coat the eggplant. Cover with plastic wrap for at least 1 hour and leave at room temperature. If you have the time, even better results come from an overnight refrigerated bath. Remove the plastic from the eggplant pieces and drain. Dredge the slices in flour and set aside on a plate.

Pour enough oil into a skillet to about ¾ inch in depth. Heat the oil to 360°F over medium heat. If you do not have a thermometer, one handy trick is to use a wooden chopstick. As the oil heats, touch the tip of the chopstick to the bottom of the skillet at an angle. Once you see lots of bubbles forming around the entirety of the submerged chopstick, the oil is ready.

Prepare a wire rack over a baking sheet and place it next to the stove. Carefully place a few eggplant pieces into the hot oil one at a time, being sure not to overcrowd the skillet. Fry the eggplant for 4 to 5 minutes, turning occasionally, until golden brown and cooked through. Remove the fried eggplant pieces to the wire rack. Repeat with the remaining eggplant.

Transfer the fried eggplant to a platter in a single layer or slightly overlapping. Drizzle with molasses and serve hot.

"Who would imagine they would have whiskey up here, he thought. But La Granja was the most likely place in Spain to find it when you thought it over. Imagine Sordo getting a bottle for the visiting dynamiter and then remembering to bring it down and leave it . . . . Remembering to bring the whiskey was one of the reasons you loved these people."

—*For Whom the Bell Tolls*

SOLOMILLO AL WHISKEY

Pork Tenderloin with Whiskey Sauce

TOTAL TIME: 25 minutes
SERVES: 2 to 3 as an entrée

Whiskey sauce on a steak, pork, and even a *tortilla española* is a very Andalusian treat. But, whiskey itself is not top-of-mind on the Spanish spectrum of drink. So, why this sauce? Whiskey producers from Northern Europe would age their liquor in sherry casks, and if times were lean, they would trade whiskey for the finest barrels from Andalusia. With a glut of whiskey around, regional chefs put the booze to use in creative ways, this sauce chief among them.

One 8-ounce pork tenderloin, sliced into ½-inch rounds

1 teaspoon kosher salt

¼ teaspoon freshly ground black pepper

¼ cup extra-virgin olive oil

6 cloves garlic, minced

1 tablespoon all-purpose flour

2 tablespoons freshly squeezed lemon juice

1 cup whiskey

1 cup chicken stock

Season the pork with ½ teaspoon of the salt and the pepper. Add the olive oil and garlic to a skillet over medium-high heat. Swirl the garlic around while the oil heats. When the oil begins to shimmer, add the pork and sauté it on both sides, about 2 to 3 minutes total. Transfer the pork to a plate and leave the accumulated juices and garlic in the pan.

Whisk the flour into the liquid and cook for 1 minute. Add the lemon juice, whiskey, stock, and the remaining ½ teaspoon of salt and bring to a boil. Whisk to maintain a smooth sauce and allow the sauce to reduce for 5 minutes. Add the seared pork back to the skillet, reduce the heat to medium-low, and simmer for an additional 5 minutes. Discard the garlic.

Serve the pork on a platter smothered with sauce, alongside rice, bread, or, traditionally, French fries.

"Toi and moi have lived through about as bad times as ever were. I don't mean just wars. Wars are spinach. Life in general is the tough part."

—LETTER TO MARLENE DIETRICH, 1950

ESPINACAS CON GARBANZOS

Spinach and Chickpeas

TOTAL TIME: 30 minutes
SERVES: 4 to 6 as a tapa

The combination of spinach, chickpeas, and warming spices like cumin and paprika has deeply Moorish origins. In the Muslim kitchen, vegetables with a protein plus flavorful additions frequently stood in where meat may have been forbidden, short-lived, or too expensive. When the Moors, and therefore this dish, came to Spain, it gained in popularity among non-Muslims as well for times like Lent, where deliciousness and avoidance of meat were key.

¼ cup extra-virgin olive oil, plus more for drizzling

1 small onion, diced

1 medium tomato, halved, stemmed, grated, and skin discarded

5 cloves garlic, minced

1 teaspoon ground cumin

2 teaspoons smoked paprika

½ teaspoon kosher salt

¼ teaspoon freshly ground black pepper

6 ounces fresh baby spinach

One 14-ounce can chickpeas, drained and rinsed

Crusty bread, for serving

Add the olive oil to a skillet over medium heat. When the oil begins to shimmer, add the onion and sauté for 8 to 10 minutes, until it is translucent. Add the tomato, garlic, cumin, paprika, salt, and pepper and continue to sauté until very fragrant, about 1 to 2 minutes more.

Add the spinach in handfuls and stir in until the leaves wilt. When all of the spinach is wilted, continue to sauté until the leaves have released their water and it has evaporated, about 3 to 4 minutes. Reduce the heat, stir in ¼ cup of water and the chickpeas, and continue to sauté until the mixture has darkened slightly and thickened, about 8 to 10 minutes.

Transfer the mixture to a serving bowl, drizzle with additional olive oil, and serve hot with crusty bread.

"Never have I seen a banquet at which a higher pitch of real flamenco enthusiasm was reached and yet we had not arrived at the unveiling of the bull's head which was, after all, the reason for the celebration of the banquet."

—FOR WHOM THE BELL TOLLS

FLAMENQUÍN
Chicken Roulade

TOTAL TIME: 2 hours, 30 minutes
SERVES: 5 to 7 as a tapa, 4 as an entrée

Just as with flamenco dance, theories abound for the origin of this dish's name. Some say it means "little Flemish," referring to the tall, thin, blond guards from Northern Belgium employed by King Carlos I. Some say it stems from the Arabic term for nomadic peasants. Still others lean on Latin and the word for flame. The least likely theory, but the funniest, is that the *Flamenquín* roll looks like the slender leg of one of the dancers.

CHICKEN ROULADE

Two 6- to 8-ounce boneless, skinless chicken breasts

2 cloves garlic, minced

2 tablespoons dried parsley

1 teaspoon kosher salt

2 tablespoons freshly squeezed lemon juice

4 ounces Spanish ham or *Jamón Ibérico*, thinly sliced

4 ounces Gruyère cheese, cut into ½-inch batons

1 cup all-purpose flour

2 eggs, beaten with 1 tablespoon of water

1 cup dried breadcrumbs

Extra-virgin olive oil, for frying

TOMATO-CARAMEL SAUCE

1 cup sugar

1 cup cherry tomatoes, halved

¼ teaspoon kosher salt

TO PREPARE THE CHICKEN: Cut each breast half into 2 flat fillets. Place the fillets between 2 sheets of plastic or parchment. Pound them with a meat mallet into even ¼-inch slabs. Transfer the chicken to a bowl and evenly mix with garlic, parsley, salt, and lemon juice. Cover and set aside for 2 hours or refrigerate overnight.

TO MAKE THE TOMATO-CARAMEL SAUCE: In a heavy-bottomed, high-sided pot over medium heat, combine the sugar with ¼ cup of water and stir until the sugar has dissolved. Add the tomatoes and salt and continue to stir until the tomatoes have softened and the skins have detached. Strain the sauce into a bowl and rewarm when the roulades are being fried.

TO MAKE THE ROULADES: Remove the chicken from the fridge and lay the fillets flat on a work surface. Cover the fillets with a thin layer of ham and then place cheese sticks down one of the long sides of the fillet atop the ham. Carefully roll the chicken and ham around the cheese like a poster, such that the outer layer of the roll is only chicken. Roll each roulade in flour, then egg wash, then breadcrumbs, and set aside on a plate.

Pour enough oil into a skillet to about 1 inch in depth. Heat the oil to 350°F over medium heat. If you do not have a thermometer, one handy trick is to use a wooden chopstick. As the oil heats, touch the tip of the chopstick to the bottom of the skillet at an angle. Once you see lots of bubbles forming around the entirety of the submerged chopstick, the oil is ready.

Prepare a wire rack over a baking sheet and place it next to the stove. Carefully place each roulade into the hot oil. Work in batches and do not overcrowd the pan. Fry each roulade until golden brown, turning occasionally, about 4 to 6 minutes in total. Remove the roulades to the wire rack and repeat until all are fried.

If serving the roulades as a tapa, slice each one into 3 to 4 rounds. Serve hot, glazed with the tomato-caramel sauce. French fries are often served on the side.

CHAPTER 8

MORNING WALK

The People's Breakfast

"If they are not good at their trade they are a definite liability to the matador and are expensive at any price, but as it is, no matter how good they become at their profession, they cannot become more than day laborers compared to the matadors."

—*Death in the Afternoon*

The sun wakes us, though it seems gentler here. The haze of last night, crispy things, cold beer, and camaraderie fades fast. Again, we follow Hemingway's lead of rising with the sun, but not to write. We walk this city to find its pulse in the people who live here. Those who sweep the dust from the arena seats, who clear the streets of yesterday's revelry, who deliver the food, the wine, the news. These are the ones we want to meet. The ones who keep it all moving, keep it real.

We start near the bullring, drawn to the belly of the beast, as it were, but not for a fight. The streets are quiet, save for the scrape of brooms, orange trees just breathing their scent, and the low rumble of delivery carts and trucks. These men and women are tired, but there's life in their steps. We follow them and the smell of coffee and bread to Casa Moreno. It's hidden behind the facade of a shop, but the small bar inside is alive at this hour.

The bite is simple. *Pan con Tomate* (page 81), bread toasted just right, rubbed with garlic, anointed with the best olive oil, and smeared with freshly grated tomato. Touch of salt. Sevilla loves her toast. Here the worship of barely charred bread is on display as the rolling toaster is Casa Moreno's busiest cooking machine on any given day.

Not enough is said about Spain's preoccupation with olive oil. They beat the rest of the world in this obsession, it's been said. A Spaniard will drizzle this liquid gold on everything, except maybe their coffee. Another adornment is set aside for that. We receive our *café bombón*. A coffee that at first is two-toned, black with creamy white. It thickens as we stir in the condensed milk, the combination a "luxury" in *For Whom the Bell Tolls*. The cup offers the kind of jolt that wakes you up, but your head is still on a pillow.

The workers at the counter eat quickly and talk faster. Most take a moment to offer us a *"buenos dias"* and wonder about our trade. Lively bunch, some with morning shots of an herbal liqueur. Their shifts maybe ending, or maybe beginning, but there's a shared rhythm here. An honesty. Hemingway virtues. A place for good food to fuel good honorable work. No show but for the photos of bullfights and Easter processions lining the walls. Both as religious.

Hemingway wrote, "I would walk along the quais when I had finished work or when I was trying to think something out. It was easier to think if I was walking and doing something or seeing people doing something that they understood." So, we walk the river still watching those who give the city life. The water is wide and steady, its banks alive with morning joggers, moans of ferry boats, and visitors like us.

We happen upon a replica of one of Magellan's ships, small and sturdy, a symbol of what one can endure when they have the will for it. Magellan had vision. He never made it home, but Juan Sebastián Elcano did, with eighteen men and the story of a world circled. Hemingway would have celebrated them both, though perhaps more for Elcano, the unsung hero who finished what another started.

From the river, we wander toward the cathedral. Its spires cut the blue sky. We come not for the view, but for a grounding thought. Inside lies Columbus, carried by sculpted men of bronze who seem to strain under his weight. Hemingway heralded men of action, but famously despised misplaced mythology. And here it is a thug in fine clothes. Columbus opened up a world with cruel methods and a criminal crew. But, thank you, Chris, for the tomatoes. We head back to the river.

"This honor thing is not some fantasy that I am trying to inflict on you in the way writers on the peninsula give out their theories on its people. I swear it is true. Honor to a Spaniard, no matter how dishonest, is as real a thing as water, wine, or olive oil."

—*Death in the Afternoon*

PAN CON TOMATE

Toast with Tomato Smear

TOTAL TIME: 10 minutes

SERVES: 6 to 8 as a tapa or an appetizer, 4 as an entrée

Spanish cuisine, if nothing else, is deceptively simple. At times, it takes only a few of the right ingredients to expose its true complexity. Tomato bread is a great example. Equal parts bright, sweet, salty, and umami-forward. Rustic and accessible yet sophisticated on the tongue. Crispy, chewy, wet, then dry. Bread with tomato smear is, in many important ways, perfect. Texture, aroma, flavor, and mouthfeel, all in harmony.

3 medium, ripe tomatoes, halved, stemmed, grated, and skins discarded

¼ cup extra-virgin olive oil

½ teaspoon kosher salt

4 ciabatta rolls, halved

Preheat the oven to 400°F.

Briskly whisk together the grated tomato, olive oil, and salt. Place the split rolls onto a baking sheet, crust-side down. Rub the tomato smear evenly across the tops of the bread. Transfer the pan to the oven and toast in the oven for 6 to 8 minutes.

Serve hot, open-face as a tapa or an appetizer, or sandwich the smeared top and bottom of a roll for an entrée.

CHAPTER 9

THE PASSION

One Holy Meal

"Our nada who art in nada, nada be thy name thy kingdom nada thy will be nada in nada as it is in nada. Give us this nada our daily nada and nada us our nada as we nada our nadas and nada us not into nada but deliver us from nada; pues nada. Hail nothing full of nothing, nothing is with thee. He smiled and stood before a bar with a shining steam pressure coffee machine."

—"A CLEAN, WELL-LIGHTED PLACE"

Now filled with our holy trinity of bread, tomato, and coffee, we sit for a spell by the Guadalquivir and watch the final throes of morning unfold. Like the river's current, dark and steady under a still cloudy sky, shops open their gates, the barbers of Sevilla take their first snips, and life begins in earnest. The Maestranza bullring looms over our shoulders, a silent monument to Hemingway's inner dissonance. He sparred with the *Sevillanos* over their handling of the *corrida*, disillusioned by the politics over the art. Yet, even in his critique, he found something to admire, their passion. It wasn't pure, but it was undeniable, native even, and for Hemingway, that kind of devotion mattered.

To Hemingway, Sevilla was a city of rituals, of processions and sacred rhythms. He was drawn to the city for the April festival, the Andalusian capital at its best, the time of *Semana Santa*, Holy Week. In the voice of Jake Barnes, Hemingway wrote, "I was a little ashamed, and regretted that I was such a rotten Catholic, but realized there was nothing I could do about it, at least for a while, and maybe never, but that anyway it was a grand religion." He admired the Andalusians for such grandeur. Especially during the festival. A lunch of the Lenten sort seems in order, the kind you'd get right before Easter. Something without meat, an offering, a nod to God in this devout town.

We leave the river behind and head toward a sanctuary about as old as the cathedral, the church of Santa Catalina. It is named for the same saint as that celebrity island off Los Angeles, where it was rumored Hemingway first conceived of the story of *The Old Man and the Sea*. Not true, but we enjoy a good rumor. We head in and light a candle and with it some incense. There is something mystical about Sevilla. Who knows if we have something that needs forgiving, but it seems possible.

El Rinconcillo is across the alleyway, the city's longest-living bar at around 350 years young. A place to seek penance of a different sort. The tables and chairs made of wood reminiscent of pews. Tiled walls of blues, reds, and greens, clearly the work of Triana artisans across the river. The aroma of olive oil instead of frankincense, but nevertheless a temple to what is good, Hemingway's ghost among the parishioners. Their menu is not thick but big on quality, with plenty of dishes that at least *feel like* giving something up.

The first dish arrives, *Salmorejo* (page 85). A chilled, smooth tomato soup thickened with bread, enriched with olive oil, with bits of ham and egg. The kind of food Hemingway appreciated for its simplicity and purpose. Like gazpacho, *salmorejo* offers yet another way for a guy like Hemingway to drink his vegetables, and what was the man

without his drink? Speaking of which, Hemingway once said, "I gave up expensive wines for Lent of 1947, and never took it up again." So, we order a cheap bottle of Valdepeñas and alternate sips of wine and of soup.

Next, though the *salmorejo* hits the mark for tasting of earth and sun, we crave the char of the grill. A plate of perfectly fired produce of the season arrives to take the edge off. It's not a steak, but it will do. Mushrooms, zucchini, eggplant, peppers, and asparagus that offer the interactive portion of lunch, as we self-administer sherry vinegar and the best olive oil that Andalusia squeezes out. Hemingway had a thing for unadorned, elemental cooking, especially of the Mediterranean variety, touched by fire.

The main course is *Bacalao con Tomate* (page 89), salt-cod simmered in a tomato sauce that clings to the fish in thick, ruby-red folds. Cod has a connection to Lent; it's plentiful, and since it's preserved without refrigeration, it's available unlike any other fish. It offers a way of being a good Catholic during Lent, and swimming in a tomato bath is as Lenten as any dish can get. Cod is sacrificial, eaten with regard to both God and tradition. But we felt no sacrifice and ate the dish with deserved reverence.

The family at the next table catches our eye. They seem to be on the same path, a meatless meal, or maybe they're taking a cue from us. Their table holds the same dishes as ours. Perhaps they know El Rinconcillo's hand at these Lenten staples, or maybe it's just luck. They pause to pray before their wine, heads bowed in quiet reflection. The youngest, Jaime, about four, clutches a toy with the worship of a matador holding his cape. Though, he drops it often, and we retrieve it, each time earning his wide-eyed gratitude and a laugh.

Our waiter, who has been shepherding us through a meal that no longer feels of austerity, delivers our dessert with the expected short tale. *Torrijas* (page 86), slices of day-old bread, soaked in milk and sugar, fried to golden perfection and served atop a crumble of some kind and a scoop of hazelnut ice cream. This, he says, as Hemingway may have quipped, is the sweet crispy body of Christ, a traditional and fitting end to our Lenten meal.

As we sip strong coffee to finish, the bar begins to fill with *Sevillanos*, their voices rising and falling in the easy cadence of a city at peace with itself. Hemingway once noted that the rituals of the bullfight were as much for the audience as for the matador. The same could be said of Sevilla's religious traditions, the processions, the fasting. The meals prepared by passionate chefs shared at tables like this one, each an act of devotion for the cook and for the diner. Binding people to their history and to each other. It is time for a siesta.

"He had meant to have a great afternoon, and instead it was an afternoon of sneers, shouted insults, and finally a volley of cushions and pieces of bread and vegetables, thrown down at him in the plaza where he had had his greatest triumphs."

—*The Sun Also Rises*

SALMOREJO
Chilled Tomato Soup

TOTAL TIME: 1 hour, 10 minutes
SERVES: 4 to 6 as a tapa or an appetizer

Salmorejo, that cold soup, cousin to gazpacho, may just be the culmination of all the cultures that worked their way across the Iberian Peninsula over centuries. Neolithic farmers figured out how to break down produce into edible portions. Roman armies subsisted on soups made with old bread. The Moors brought spices to the table. And, for all its questionable methods, the Columbian Exchange brought the tomatoes.

- 4 large ripe tomatoes, halved and cored
- One 8-to-10-ounce day-old baguette or other stale bread, crusts removed
- 1 clove garlic
- 2 tablespoons sherry vinegar
- ¼ teaspoon kosher salt
- 1 cup extra-virgin olive oil
- 2 hard-boiled eggs, diced (optional)
- 4 ounces Spanish ham or *Jamón Ibérico*, diced (optional)

To a blender, add the tomatoes and purée for 2 minutes, until smooth. Tear the bread into hunks and add them to the blender, along with the garlic, vinegar, and salt. Purée for 2 to 3 minutes, until smooth. Slowly drizzle in the olive oil and continue to purée. Adjust the salt to taste. Pass the resulting *salmorejo* through a fine-mesh strainer into a container. Cover and refrigerate for at least 1 hour.

Remove the *salmorejo* from the refrigerator. To serve, portion the soup into bowls and optionally garnish with diced egg and ham. Alternatively, serve as a tapa in small glasses with less garnish.

"The country was a rich coastal plain that ran from the sea to the foothills. We drove past the dark trunks and varying greens of orange and lemon trees and the silvery green of olive orchards and the houses were white and framed by palms and rows of cypresses."

—THE DANGEROUS SUMMER

TORRIJAS
French Toast

TOTAL TIME: 1 hour
SERVES: 4 to 6 as a dessert

Here is another dish that shares DNA across eras in Spain. It began with the Roman penchant for resuscitating old bread; continued through the Moors bringing cinnamon to the Peninsula; then the Catholics chimed in that sugary, hefty, fried bread would be a great way to avoid meat during high holy days; and then there's always the French across the border making the strikingly similar *pan perdú*. Okay, *torrijas* is French toast.

TORRIJAS

4 cups whole milk

½ cup sugar

1 cinnamon stick

1-inch-wide strip lemon peel

1-inch-wide strip orange peel

1 pound day-old baguette, bias-cut into 1-inch-thick slices

4 large eggs

¼ teaspoon kosher salt

Extra-virgin olive oil, for frying

CRUMBLE AND TO SERVE

⅓ cup light brown sugar, packed

½ teaspoon ground cinnamon

¼ cup unsalted butter, melted

¾ cup all-purpose flour

6 scoops preferred ice cream

TO START THE TORRIJAS: In a pot on the stove over medium-high heat, add the milk, sugar, cinnamon, and lemon and orange peel. Whisk regularly until the sugar has dissolved. When the mixture begins to simmer, reduce the heat to low and continue to simmer for 20 minutes. Remove from the heat and allow it to cool while preparing the crumble.

TO MAKE THE CRUMBLE: Preheat the oven to 350°F.

In a small bowl, combine the brown sugar and cinnamon, then smoothly stir in the melted butter. Stir in the flour, then use clean hands to form the mixture into pea-size crumbs. Spread the crumb mixture onto a parchment- or silicone-lined baking sheet and transfer to the oven for 10 minutes. Remove from the oven and redistribute the crumble into even crumbs, then return to the oven for 5 minutes. Remove from the oven and set aside to cool.

TO FINISH THE TORRIJAS: Prepare a wire rack over a baking sheet. Remove the citrus peels and cinnamon stick from the milk mixture. Soak the bread slices in the milk mixture, several at a time, until saturated but not soggy. Each slice should feel like a medium-wet sponge. Place the soaked slices on the wire rack and allow them to rest for 10 minutes.

In a shallow bowl, briskly whisk the eggs with the salt. Add oil to a skillet over medium-high heat. Ideally, the oil comes up to about half an inch in the pan. When the oil begins to shimmer, take 1 slice of bread and dip each edge into the egg mixture, then gently lower it into the hot oil. In small batches, fry on one side for about 90 seconds, until the bread is beginning to brown, followed by the other side for an additional 90 seconds. Remove to a paper-towel-lined plate. Repeat for the remaining bread slices.

Serve *torrijas* hot, sitting atop the cinnamon crumble, alongside a scoop of great ice cream.

"I will obtain olives and salted codfish and hazel nuts for thee to eat while thou drinkest and we will stay in the room for a month and never leave it."

—*For Whom the Bell Tolls*

BACALAO CON TOMATE

Salt-Cod in Tomato Sauce

TOTAL TIME: 1 hour, 35 minutes, plus desalting time, if using salt-cod
SERVES: 3 to 4 as a tapa or an appetizer, 1 to 2 as an entrée

It was Basque fishers who first figured out how to use salt to preserve their vast cod hauls for transport and business across Spain. The Basque technique was adopted by other European cultures, but nowhere in the world does salt-cod reign supreme but in Spain and Portugal. It provided a cheap, year-round, reliable source of protein and therefore spawned scores of culinary uses over time. *Bacalao* is a good friend to tomato.

- 8 to 10 ounces salt-cod fillet, ideally center cut
- ½ cup all-purpose flour
- ⅔ cup extra-virgin olive oil
- 1 small onion, diced
- 1 red bell pepper, cored and diced
- 3 cloves garlic, minced
- One 14-ounce can tomato purée
- ½ teaspoon kosher salt
- ¼ teaspoon freshly ground black pepper
- ½ teaspoon sugar
- 2 tablespoons minced parsley, for garnish
- Crusty bread, rice, potatoes, or pasta, for serving

Under cold running water, rinse the exterior salt from the salt-cod. In a large bowl, cover the salt-cod with more cold water, cover the bowl, and refrigerate for 36 hours, replacing the water 3 times through the duration.

Remove the cod from the refrigerator, rinse off any remaining surface salt, and dry thoroughly with paper towels. Dredge the cod in flour and set aside.

Add ⅓ cup of the olive oil to a skillet over medium heat. When the oil begins to shimmer, add the cod and slowly sauté it for 4 to 6 minutes, until lightly browned. Flip the cod and continue to sauté until just cooked through, about 3 to 5 minutes. Remove the cod from skillet and set aside on paper towels.

Add the remaining ⅓ cup of olive oil to the skillet over medium heat. When the oil begins to shimmer, add the onion and bell pepper and sauté for 7 to 8 minutes, until the onion is translucent. Add the garlic and continue to sauté for 1 to 2 minutes, until very fragrant. Pour in the tomato purée, and stir in the salt, pepper, and sugar. Reduce the heat to low, cover the skillet, and allow the sauce to cook for 5 minutes.

Uncover the skillet and add the cooked cod into the sauce, spooning some over the fish. Cover the skillet and allow the sauce and fish to cook for an additional 5 minutes.

Serve the sauced cod hot, topped with parsley, along with crusty bread, rice, potatoes, or pasta.

NOTE ABOUT SALT-COD: *As a substitute, you may use fresh cod that has been seasoned with 1 teaspoon of kosher salt for every 1 pound of fish and set aside for 1 hour. In this case, skip the soaking and rinsing steps and simply use the seasoned fresh fish in the recipe. The texture will not be as meaty as salt-cod, but the overall effect is maintained.*

CHAPTER 10

THE BULL

A VIP Dinner

"Neither of us cared truly for Sevilla. This is heresy in Andalusia and in bullfighting. People who care about bullfighting are supposed to have a mystic feeling about Sevilla."

—*The Dangerous Summer*

The Maestranza sits white and gold in the early-evening sun, its shadows stretching like the memory of the bulls that bled within its walls. Hemingway called this "majestic plaza" the most beautiful, a spiritual capital of the art, home to talented and worshiped matadors, but wrote, too, of its tragedy, and of the corrupt hands that could ruin it all. Sevilla's bullring had turned on him, or he on it, but no matter. We are here, as he had been, to reckon with the art, the blood, and the sacrifice.

We continue on a path that we began back in Madrid. To honor the bull rather than anyone else in the ring, and that path feels truer here than elsewhere. And if Hemingway were persona non grata to the VIP echelon of Sevilla bullfighting, we may as well surround ourselves with the luxuries that we can. We head to Palo Cortao, the finest sherry bar that Hemingway never met. We hear that Ana and Chef Ángel, the proprietors, are the Sherpas of sherry and show us the ways of the grape.

Here, the gift of sherry always softened harder truths. For Hemingway, sherry was the essence of Spain captured in a bottle. The craftsmanship, the depth, the dedication. It becomes our companion for the evening, a liquid reverence for the traditions that lingered, even if the purity of the *corrida* had been sullied for Hemingway. Sherry always treated him right. We sit on the terrace just inside an alley, steps away from a bustling Sevilla returning home from work. Somehow, it's quieter here. The dwindling sunlight struggles to round the corner of the boulevard into our sanctuary, as Ana slides our first pour, our lightest, a Manzanilla. Crisp and dry, Hemingway's favorite, it tastes of that same dwindling sun.

The beef will come, and that moment will be good, but like a Manzanilla, an awakening start to any meal in Spain was *sopa*. Palo Cortao with Chef Ángel at the stove is known for an Andalusian classic, their *Ajo Blanco* (page 95), garlic and almond soup. As it arrives, a waiter drizzles, with precision, this white gold atop a tartare of mango and salmon. It is as beautiful a bowl as it is aromatic. There is a faint coconut aura and it tastes of good olive oil and the almonds we expect, punctuated by a dollop of caviar. Hemingway believed in the simplicity of Spanish cuisine, but the adornments here become the fabric of the dish, not mere decoration.

Ana returns with the second glass, a *fino*, slightly browner than the Manzanilla, still dry and a little briny, which met the *ajo blanco* well. Like a favorite character in a stage play who makes their big splash in the second act, the salmon sings along with the *fino*. La Venencia in Madrid certainly has its history and certain allure, but this food with this drink on this terrace is a far cry from old wood and secrets. No, this place Hemingway would have approved, with excellent food, quality drink, and affable hosts. The Spanish trifecta.

Then the main event begins. *Tartar de Toro con Tuetano* (page 92). On a single platter arrives the roasted marrow in all its richness served alongside a bowl of beef tartare. The marrow glistens in its bone, hot and melting. The tartare, a fitting tribute to Hemingway's Paris days with Hadley. As Ana arrives timed for the plate with a glass of amontillado, she suggests the proper delivery. Marrow like butter on a small slice of toast, followed by tartare. A sip of the sherry cuts the fattiness and exposes the depth of the finely cut fillet. Perfect, bright, indulgent, almost primal.

We enjoy a brief taste of oloroso, a darker sherry, richer, more reflective before the surprise glass of the night and what would be Hemingway's honor. The namesake sip of the restaurant, *palo cortado*. They say it is the rarest of the sherries and mysterious. Its arrival on the table seems to dull the noise of a growing crowd, as though the weight of the drink demanded silence. Complex, buttery, and deep with a lingering on the tongue. It is good and brings our learning with Ana to an ideal close.

The night cools as we step out onto the cobbled streets, Sevilla alive around us with its chatter and motion. The sherry smoothed the edges, but the city remains sharp, a place of beauty, conflict, and devotion. For all its flaws, Hemingway couldn't quite turn away, and neither could we. Until morning, that is, and our journey to Ronda and beyond.

"The proprietor, who was a short, middle-aged man, heavily built and square faced, had come over. 'He thinks we ought to have meat of some kind.'"

—*The Garden of Eden*

TARTAR DE TORO CON TUETANO

Beef Tartare with Bone Marrow

TOTAL TIME: 30 minutes
SERVES: 6 to 8 as a tapa or an appetizer

Beef tartare is thought to have been an innovation among Central Asian warriors and herdsmen as they placed raw meat under their saddles to tenderize it as they galloped. Eventually, this loose technique was refined and codified by nineteenth-century French chefs who likely never met a Central Asian herdsman, and word spread over the Pyrenees. Like other French recipes, tartar caught on like wildfire in Spain.

MARROW BONE

One 2-to-3-pound beef-marrow bone, split lengthwise by a butcher

½ teaspoon kosher salt

¼ teaspoon freshly ground black pepper

BEEF TARTARE

1 pound beef tenderloin, diced

¼ cup coarsely chopped chives

2 tablespoons capers, minced

¼ cup extra-virgin olive oil

1 tablespoon soy sauce

1 egg yolk

1 tablespoon Dijon or other whole-grain mustard

½ teaspoon kosher salt

¼ teaspoon freshly ground black pepper

Toast points, for serving

TO MAKE THE MARROW BONE: Preheat the oven to 450°F. Season the top of the flat side of the split bone with salt and pepper. Transfer to a baking sheet and roast in the oven for 15 to 25 minutes, depending on the size of the bone. When the top of the marrow looks to be bubbling a bit, it is cooked. While the bone is roasting, make the tartare. Remove from the oven and serve hot.

TO MAKE THE BEEF TARTARE: Stir all the ingredients together in a mixing bowl, then transfer them to a serving bowl. Serve alongside the marrow bone with toast points. Suggest to guests that they use the marrow like butter on the bread before topping it with tartare.

NOTE ABOUT DICING THE BEEF: *Generally, the colder the beef, the easier it will be to cut. One tip is to freeze the steak and thaw it overnight in the refrigerator. This will leave it cold enough to dice for tartare.*

A
S
SHIFT
Z
X
C
V
B
N

"In a back room, Robert Cohn was sleeping quietly on some wine-casks. It was almost too dark to see his face. They had covered him with a coat and another coat was folded under his head. Around his neck and on his chest was a big wreath of twisted garlics."

—*The Sun Also Rises*

AJO BLANCO
Chilled White Garlic Soup

TOTAL TIME: 1 hour, 15 minutes
SERVES: 4 to 6 as a tapa or an appetizer

When we met one of the owners of Palo Cortao, Ana Hergueta, she was the host one might expect at an upscale eatery in Sevilla, affable as they come. When she heard that we'd like to learn the ins and outs of sherry, she was visibly amplified. Then, when we told her of the Hemingway project as the reason we wanted to learn, Ana was beside herself as a proud fan of his writing. Not only was Ana clearly the right host at the right time, but Palo Cortao's reason for being is their extensive list of bottles, even by Sevilla standards. Ana made sure that we came by later that night to meet Chef Ángel Alarcón, the man behind their other claim to fame, *ajo blanco* with coconut milk and salmon tartare.

SALMON AND MANGO TARTARE

1 mango, peeled and diced

4 to 6 ounces salmon, skinned and diced

1 teaspoon kimchi mayonnaise or other spicy mayonnaise

1 teaspoon teriyaki sauce

1 tablespoon extra-virgin olive oil

AJO BLANCO

1½ cups almonds

2 cloves garlic

½ apple, peeled and diced

3½ cups coconut milk

3 tablespoons apple cider vinegar

2 teaspoons kosher salt

½ cup extra-virgin olive oil

2 tablespoons chopped chives, for garnish

Black caviar, for garnish (optional)

TO MAKE THE SALMON AND MANGO TARTARE: In a mixing bowl, evenly combine all the ingredients. Cover and refrigerate until ready to use.

TO MAKE THE AJO BLANCO: Using a countertop or handheld blender, first break down the almonds and garlic into as fine a paste as possible. Then, add the apple and purée until smooth. Add the coconut milk, 1⅔ cups of water, the vinegar, and salt. Purée for 2 to 3 minutes, until smooth. Slowly drizzle in the olive oil and continue to purée. Adjust salt to taste.

Pass the resulting *ajo blanco* through a fine-mesh strainer into a container. Cover and refrigerate for at least 1 hour.

Remove the *ajo blanco* and tartare from the refrigerator. To serve, portion the tartare into the middle of bowls and pour the *ajo blanco* around it. Top with chives and caviar, if using. Alternatively, serve as a tapa in small glasses with less garnish.

CHAPTER 11

ROMANCE

Ronda Sizzles

"The entire town and as far as you can see in any direction is romantic background and there is a hotel there that is so comfortable, so well run and where you eat so well and usually have a cool breeze at night that, with the romantic background and the modern comfort, if a honeymoon or an elopement is not a success in Ronda it would be as well to start for Paris and both commence making your own friends."

—*Death in the Afternoon*

Hemingway loved Ronda. Everything he admired about Spain, everything that stirred him and stayed with him seemed to come together here. It could have been the legend of Pedro Romero who changed bullfighting forever when he faced the bull on foot instead of steed. Or the Ordoñez men, father and son, masters of the ring and friends of his. Maybe it was this, the oldest bullring in Spain, the place where the *corrida* felt truer than anywhere else. The views that stopped you in your tracks. The romance. The stillness of the air. The comfort of knowing Sevilla was behind you, not far but far enough. There was no question. When we left the Alfonso XIII this morning, the car pointed toward Ronda, and lunch.

He knew this town on the edge of the cliff well. He also knew the cliff. Knew it for the romantic views, knew it as a place to throw fascists to their death, for the tragedy of horses losing to a bull and being dragged over. We could see the town knew Hemingway too, as we walk past the monument to him behind the bullring, across the gravel path from a matching tribute to Ronda's other foreign son, Orson Welles. One imagines the duo in afterlife fisticuffs over who got the prime position or the bigger stone.

Our first good view of the El Tajo gorge and the arched bridge is perched atop the Mirador de Hemingway, a vista point that he was known to have loved and where he escorted a paramour or a few. Then there is a hotel that came to be well after he lived, the Hemingway Palace, with ample and era-appropriate memorabilia, shelves of books, and one excellent restaurant, Pura Cepa. He once wrote in *The Toronto Star*, "I have discovered that there is romance in food when romance has disappeared from everywhere else." With a paramour nowhere in sight, we think about a lunch that may pinch-hit for a lusty affair.

Our time is shorter than most other days and other meals and there is the long haul to Valencia after we're done. We order everything at once and it arrives quickly, a feast fit for lovers with a deadline. *Gambas al Ajillo* (page 98), a sultry symbol of Hemingway's fantasy, the *Royal Order of Shrimp Eaters*. The naked crustaceans come out hot, still sizzling in their oil, garlic sharp in the air. One could hear the heat of it, taste the sea in the flesh. It is the kind of dish that begs you to lean in closer, ignoring the obvious danger.

Pimientos del Padrón Fritos (page 97). The peppers, fried until they blistered, soft and green, the kind that melted on the tongue, except when they didn't. Every so often, one of them came with spicy tinge. Unexpected, like a caress you weren't ready for but didn't want to refuse. We keep eating them, anyway, daring the next one to surprise again.

Last, *Chuletas de Cordero a la Parrilla* (page 101), simply grilled lamb chops. They are charred at the edges, the meat warm and red. We eat them as one would a lollipop with a bone for a stick, the juices dripping down our wrists. This is carnal, primal like the smell of fire or the feel of skin against skin. There was no talking, only the sound of teeth on bone.

With stomachs full and a sated feeling, Ronda did us an afternoon right, but the road is calling. Valencia is waiting with its own promises, its own stories. This town, like a love long-lost, left us wanting more.

"When I was a small kid I would only eat meat and fish. They couldn't get me to eat vegetables . . ."

—LETTER TO CHARLES SCRIBNER, 1951

PIMIENTOS DEL PADRÓN FRITOS
Blistered Padrón Peppers

TOTAL TIME: 5 minutes
SERVES: 4 to 6 as a tapa or an appetizer

Unlike the sweet *piquillo* peppers that arrived in Navarra during the Colombian Exchange, smaller green peppers were brought to Padrón, Galicia, by Franciscan monks a century later. Speculative, but perhaps they embraced the mystery of the fruit's sometimes sweet and sometimes quite spicy character. A little surprising thrill for this monastic bunch.

2 tablespoons vegetable oil
12 ounces green Padrón or shishito peppers
2 tablespoons extra-virgin olive oil
½ teaspoon kosher salt

Add the oil to a cast-iron skillet over high heat. When the oil begins to smoke slightly, add the peppers in a single layer and allow them to cook on one side for 45 to 60 seconds, until slightly charred and blistered. Flip the peppers and cook for another 30 to 45 seconds, until equally charred. Remove the peppers to a paper-towel-lined plate to drain excess oil.

Transfer the peppers to a serving platter, drizzle with extra-virgin olive oil, sprinkle with salt, and serve hot.

"'Tell him all about your bull-fighter,' Mike said. 'Oh, to hell with your bull-fighter!' He tipped the table so that all the beers and the dish of shrimps went over in a crash."

—*The Sun Also Rises*

GAMBAS AL AJILLO

Sizzling Garlic Shrimp

TOTAL TIME: 40 minutes

SERVES: 3 to 4 as a tapa or an appetizer

Here is another case of simple ingredients matched with other simple ingredients to taste brilliant. Southern Spain, with its ample seafood, excellent olive oil, garlic, chiles, and lemon, is home to a good number of similar recipes. *Gambas al ajillo* is a tapas bar classic, mainly due to its quick preparation and robust results, not to mention how delicious the bread dipped into the residual sauce is.

8 ounces medium shrimp, peeled and deveined

½ teaspoon kosher salt

1 dash baking soda

½ cup plus 1 tablespoon extra-virgin olive oil, divided

4 cloves garlic, thinly sliced

½ teaspoon red pepper flakes

2 tablespoons coarsely chopped parsley

2 tablespoons freshly squeezed lemon juice

Crusty bread, for dipping

In a mixing bowl, combine the shrimp, salt, baking soda, and 1 tablespoon of the olive oil. Allow the shrimp to marinate for 30 minutes.

Add the remaining ½ cup of olive oil, the garlic, and the chile flakes to a skillet over medium-high heat. When the oil begins to bubble intensely around the garlic, stir in the marinated shrimp and sauté for 3 to 5 minutes, until the shrimp are pink and just beginning to brown at the edges.

Remove from the heat, and serve while still sizzling in the skillet, or transfer to a serving bowl. Top with parsley, drizzle on lemon juice, and serve alongside crusty bread for dipping.

"What I really like is good fresh fish, grilled, good steaks (not those comic steaks they have bred so they have no taste, but only size) with the bone and very rare. Good lamb, rare."

—LETTER TO CHARLES SCRIBNER, 1951

CHULETAS DE CORDERO A LA PARRILLA
Grilled Lamb Chops

TOTAL TIME: 1 hour, 25 minutes
SERVES: 6 as an entrée

Just as suckling pig cooked over an open fire was popularized over centuries in what became Spain, alfresco lamb preparations have a long, deep history. Domesticated pigs made their debut with the Romans, but sheep herding was prehistoric, and lamb and mutton were also much more popular meats than pork during the Moor's dominance of the peninsula.

- Six 1-inch-thick lamb loin chops
- 1½ tablespoons kosher salt
- 2 tablespoons extra-virgin olive oil
- 1 teaspoon freshly ground black pepper
- 1 teaspoon ground cumin

Dust the chops with the salt and set on a cooling rack over a baking sheet for 1 hour.

Prepare the grill to high heat on one section and cool on the other and oil the grill grates. Brush the chops with the olive oil and season with the pepper and cumin. Set the chops on the cool section and close the lid for 5 minutes. Transfer the chops to the hot section and grill on each side with the lid closed for 2 to 3 minutes, until slightly charred.

Remove the steaks from the grill and let them rest for 10 minutes. Serve warm.

Part III
VALENCIA

CHAPTER 12

THE SEA

Paella and Beyond

"Dinner at Pepica's was wonderful. It was a big, clean, open-air place and everything was cooked in plain sight. You could pick out what you wanted to have grilled or broiled and the seafood and the Valencian rice dishes were the best on the beach . . . . You could hear the sea breaking on the beach and the lights shone on the wet sand."

—*THE DANGEROUS SUMMER*

We arrive in Valencia crumpled masses of our former selves. The ones who ate like kings in love for a moment in Ronda and the ones who well underestimated how large this country is west to east. It's late night and it is raining. Hemingway once poetically wrote, "In the rain in the rain in the rain in the rain in Spain. Does it rain in Spain?" Yes, friend. It rains.

The one bright spot was that we were about to be ushered into the hotel where Hemingway began to type his own journey with Lady Brett Ashley, Robert Cohn, and Jake Barnes. Only there is no usher, and the lobby lights flicker like something out of a horror film, the Reina Victoria Hotel is also a crumpled mass of its former self. Not everything in Spain endures, it seems. If *The Sun Also Rises* were penned here today, Mr. Barnes might well be inspired to mortally maim his rollicking cohort.

Goddamn, we hate to get wet. We forge ahead, soaked through, and find comfort in a more modern hotel just down the street. This place has no reminiscences for Hemingway, no Orson Welles cigar to light with a rifle, no en suite boxing matches. It's not of his era nor does it reflect any of the palatial facade to which he grew accustomed. But the front desk is also the bar, *and that* Hemingway would have found fit. *Gin tonic for the room, please.* Finally, in a bed made of soft dry things and good smells, after our nightcap, we sleep late the next morning. Then, the sea.

Reaching its crescendo within *The Old Man and the Sea*, Hemingway had a lifelong obsession with the ocean. It is this that pulls us into Valencia and Valencia pulls us closer to La Pepica at the beach. Hemingway was a regular when he was in town. He came for the salt air and the blue water, the promise of food that held the meeting of land and sea breeze in every bite. It is also a place where time is not of the clock but of the tide.

Pepica's once sat on the sand, and over the years was urged farther back from the waves. Still, it is the best perch, and the terrace is wide open to the sound of the shore break and the hum of people out for a stroll. Hemingway wrote of the family that ran it back in his day as if it were his own, like a great aunt who keeps trying to feed you despite any level of full. They say he once tried his hand in this kitchen with disastrous results. We chat up the chef upon walking in, but do not dare cross his threshold.

Today, there is a formality, the waitstaff is sharp and organized and moves with purpose to feed hungry strangers. The tables are pretty and white-clothed, and the chairs scrape against the patio floor as the diners lean in to spoon more crusted rice, pour their drinks, or laugh at some remembered story. In the pages of *The Dangerous Summer*, Hemingway described a long meal here with detail. It's rare that he provided such vivid marching orders, so we replay the dishes one by one, albeit adapted to a contemporary menu.

We start with *Sangría* (page 110), that fruity darling of the Spanish that may punch you when you're not looking. It pours into our glasses that catch the midday sun and lights the table in pinks and blues and optimism. It isn't just wine. It is the beach. We sip slowly, deliberately, letting the citrus and sweetness spread over our tongues, opening us for what comes next.

The first plates begin to beautify our table, each vying for attention. The little chorizo sausages, their dark red skins

charred and crisp offer the right combination of salty and fatty with just a hint of the grill's alder smoke. Next came the *Tataki de Atún* (page 106), tuna, direct from the Almadraba nets down in Cádiz, barely seared on the *plancha* and sliced, still glistening served along with a sauce inspired by Asia. Then simply grilled red prawns, plump and ruby, their shells cracking under our fingers as we peeled them and squeezed some lime.

The octopus and some peppers came last in this first round of too much food. Hemingway's chosen clams will have to wait. An expertly cooked tentacle singed until it curled like centuries of waves on sand. It is deep purple, sweet and rich and sat atop a creamy mound of potato. Hemingway said it tasted like lobster. It tastes like exemplary octopus. The *Pimientos del Piquillo Confitados* (page 111), red peppers once roasted and peeled then slightly charred in the broiler and simmered in good olive oil. This on bread captivates the imagination. Thrice-cooked peppers, much like pepper-flavored butter.

We veer slightly away from Hemingway's feast as written, where there were steaks and grilled chicken. We go straight to the rice, La Pepica's reason for opening its doors each day and Valencia defined. Hemingway once said, "In Spain, honor is a very real thing..." In Valencian kitchens, *pundonor* has its own breath. *Paella Valenciana* (page 109) stands as proof, often falling victim to less-than-honorable tweaks. Keep your chorizo, onions, and mixed seafood and meat away. True *paella Valenciana* is chicken, rabbit, butter beans, flat green beans, tomatoes, garlic, saffron, paprika, rosemary, and rice. Artichokes, only when the season allows. Simple. And it was good. We skip the snails.

After finishing lunch with all the *pundonor* Valencia could demand, we leave no room for coffee, no room for dessert, and no good reason to get back behind the wheel. The afternoon stretches ahead of us like the sand, long and uncertain, so we walk. Malvarrosa beach is close, fifteen minutes at a slow pace, the kind you keep after a meal like that. Hemingway left scores of footprints in these "miles of sand without a house," and the place still carried his shadow alongside our own.

The air is chilled, the clouds hang low, but the rain had passed in the night. A swim is an idea, though maybe not sensible. It feels as if bordering on polar-bear weather but following in his footsteps meant you don't stop for comfort and you talk polar-bear talk when faced with a polar bear. We find a soft patch of sand and practice our ursine tongue.

We sit and watch wave after wave slowly moving the seaweed along the coast, entranced by the regularity of it all. The sea doesn't care about your plans or your schedule. It moves on, relentless and eternal. There was no sign of Pilar's oxen pulling boats to shore, but the occasional bundled-up family playing soccer and the old gentleman stripping down to take a lap in the Mediterranean. He shivers, jerks, and winces and we begin to doubt or own bright ideas.

We brace ourselves for the plunge and swim as the sun nears the edge of the known sea. It's cold but not impossible, fighting the waves and the currents until we resemble the "worn-out healthy savages" of Hemingway and his band. Tired and chilled to the bone, yes, but unwilling to leave the beach behind, we've worked up enough of an appetite to dine at one of the less flashy places along the beach. We dry up fast and deliberate to stave off hypothermia.

It may have been fate, but our new seaside perch serves "*rouget* that the Spaniards call *salmonete*" on rice, along with other seafood out of their shells. This is *Arróz del Senyoret con Salmonete* (page 114), or gentleman's rice, the kind that doesn't get our hands dirty while eating. We'd also be remiss not to order some *Almejas* (page 112), those clams we ran out of steam for early in the day, better late than never. So much for detail, our fatigue overrules our desire to take useful notes.

Night settles in and the sea is dark. We walk back toward La Pepica to gather our car, the sand cool under our still bare feet. The lights from Pepica's cast long shadows, and the voices on the now-crowded terrace grow louder and then quieter with our final whiffs of salt and smoke. We drive back to the hotel. The sea gave us plenty today, but it also took. Healthy, tired savages indeed.

"We drank sangría, red wine with fresh orange and lemon juice in it, served in big pitchers and ate local sausages to start with, fresh tuna, fresh prawns, and crisp fried octopus tentacles that tasted like lobster."

—*The Dangerous Summer*

TATAKI DE ATÚN
Seared Ahi Tuna

TOTAL TIME: 40 minutes
SERVES: 4 to 5 as a tapa or an appetizer

Thanks to the Phoenicians and their fish-hunting prowess, tuna has been on Spanish plates for nearly three thousand years. Some of the oldest tuna fishing methods the world-over began in what is now southern Spain. Today, most of the big catch around Cádiz ends up on sushi counters in Japan. Still, much of the fish that remains in Spain that doesn't get canned appropriately pays tribute to those very same Japanese ways. *Tataki* is a staple at bars across the country.

SWEET SOY SAUCE

⅓ cup dark soy sauce

¼ cup dry sherry

¼ cup sugar

FOR THE QUICK AIOLI

½ cup mayonnaise

½ teaspoon garlic powder

2 teaspoons freshly squeezed lemon juice

1 dash kosher salt

SEARED TUNA

1 tablespoon extra-virgin olive oil (optional)

One 8-ounce sashimi-grade tuna steak or fillet

1 tablespoon black or white sesame seeds

Toasted slices of baguette, for serving (optional)

TO MAKE THE SWEET SOY SAUCE: Add the soy sauce, sherry, and sugar to a small pot over high heat and bring to a boil. Reduce the heat to medium-low and stir until the mixture reduces by half, about 10 to 12 minutes. Set aside to cool for 25 minutes.

TO MAKE THE QUICK AIOLI: Whisk all the ingredients together in a mixing bowl and set aside.

TO MAKE THE SEARED TUNA: Using a kitchen torch or a smoking-hot skillet over high heat with 1 tablespoon of olive oil, sear just the outside of the tuna steak, about 15 seconds per edge. Remove to a cutting board. Carve the tuna into ⅛-inch-thick slices and fan out on a platter.

Leaving the tuna on primary display, dress the platter with aioli, sweet soy sauce, and sesame seeds. Optionally, serve with toasted slices of baguette.

"Then some ate steaks and others roasted or grilled chicken with saffron yellow rice . . . It was a very moderate meal by Valencian standards and the woman who owned the place was worried that we would go away hungry. Nobody talked about bullfighting."

—*The Dangerous Summer*

PAELLA VALENCIANA
Chicken and Rabbit Rice

TOTAL TIME: 1 hour
SERVES: 3 to 4 as an entrée

Though many recognize paella as Spain's national dish, seldom is the true diversity of their rice dishes celebrated internationally. Paella is certainly iconic, but when faced with a menu that doesn't include the word, look for *arróz seco*, or dry rice, the same format as paella, but the toppings can range from whole fish and specialized seafood to various sausages and other meats. Then there's *arróz meloso*, creamy rice, *arróz caldoso*, brothy rice, *arróz al horno*, baked rice, *arróz negro*, rice dyed with squid ink, and *arróz con costra,* rice crusted with egg. Even this list is merely scratching the surface of a vast landscape.

6 ounces skinless, boneless chicken thighs, cut into ½-inch cubes

6 ounces skinless, boneless rabbit loin, cut into ½-inch cubes

3 tablespoons extra-virgin olive oil, divided

1½ teaspoons kosher salt, divided

3 teaspoons smoked paprika, divided

3 cups chicken stock

1 pinch saffron

1 medium tomato, halved, stemmed, grated, and skin discarded

6 ounces Italian flat green beans

2 cloves garlic, minced

1 cup uncooked Spanish round rice, such as *bomba* or *calasparra*

7 ounces canned butter beans, drained

1 sprig fresh rosemary

In a mixing bowl, coat chicken and rabbit pieces with 1 tablespoon of olive oil, 1 teaspoon salt, and 1 teaspoon of paprika. In a heat-proof vessel on the stove or in the microwave, heat the stock and saffron for 3 minutes. Set the marinating meat and stock aside for 30 minutes.

Add the remaining 2 tablespoons of olive oil to an 11-by-13-inch *paellera* or wide skillet over medium heat. When the oil shimmers, add the chicken and rabbit, and sauté for 4 to 5 minutes, until well browned.

Add the tomato, green beans, garlic, and the remaining ½ teaspoon of salt to the pan and sauté for 3 minutes. Add the rice and continue to sauté until the rice emits a nutty aroma, about 1 minute. Carefully pour in the saffron-infused stock and stir just once to combine evenly.

Place the butter beans and rosemary sprig across the top, increase the heat to high, and bring the liquid to a boil. Reduce the heat to medium-high and maintain a strong simmer for 10 minutes. Reduce the heat to medium-low and simmer for an additional 10 to 15 minutes, until the rice has fully absorbed the liquid and is fully cooked.

If the rice needs further cooking, but has already absorbed all the liquid, add water ¼ cup at a time and simmer until complete.

Remove the rosemary and serve the rice hot with a healthy smattering of the ingredients or hand each guest a spoon and eat directly from the pan.

"Whatever it was that makes people not worry in the times between combat there was plenty of it around that summer and it did not come in bottles although the pitchers of sangria were cold and beaded over quickly in the hot dry wind that blew all day and all night."

—*The Dangerous Summer*

SANGRÍA
Fruit-Infused Wine

TOTAL TIME: 2 hours, 15 minutes
SERVES: 5 to 7

Sangria was and is a wonderful home drink in Spain, where restaurants naturally sell it as an expected traveler refreshment. It began as a way to enhance affordable wine with fruit and ice and held the fringe benefit of cooling one off in hotter seasons. Entertaining a crowd at a house party? Sangria is a great solution. Out at a restaurant in Spain? Order a *Tinto de Verano* (page 56).

2 tablespoons sugar

4 cups fruity red wine

2 oranges, juice and strips of rind divided

1 lemon, juice and strips of rind divided

2 ounces brandy

1 cinnamon stick

Additional cut citrus fruit, for serving (optional)

Dissolve the sugar in 2 tablespoons of water in a microwave or by vigorous whisking. In a large pitcher or container, combine the wine, orange juice, lemon juice, and brandy. Add the sugar water to taste. Stir in the citrus rind strips and cinnamon stick, cover, and refrigerate for at least 2 hours.

To serve, remove the sangria from refrigerator, strain and serve chilled, optionally over ice with additional slices of citrus.

"The wife of Pablo was standing over the charcoal fire on the open fire hearth in the corner of the cave. The girl knelt by her stirring in an iron pot. She lifted the wooden spoon out and looked at Robert Jordan as he stood there in the doorway."

—*For Whom the Bell Tolls*

PIMIENTOS DEL PIQUILLO CONFITADOS

Charred Roasted Peppers

TOTAL TIME: 1 hour, 25 minutes
SERVES: 6 to 8 as a tapa or an appetizer, 3 to 4 as a side dish

Piquillo peppers are transplanted chiles from South America that flourished in the northeastern Navarra region of Spain. Like the famed Hatch chile from New Mexico, the skin of a fresh *piquillo* is like leather, so using them involves charring, peeling, seeding, and preserving the whole fruits in their own juices. Their out-of-the-jar usability makes them perfect as a garnish, but slowly poaching the peppers in extra-virgin olive oil yields an exceedingly delicate, achingly fragile, buttery accoutrement.

3 cloves garlic

½ cup extra-virgin olive oil

12 to 15 jarred *piquillo* peppers, whole or 3 red bell peppers, roasted, peeled, seeded, and cut into strips

Crusty bread, for serving

Preheat the oven to 350°F.

Place the garlic cloves and olive oil in a rimmed baking dish or oven-safe skillet. Transfer into the oven and roast for 15 to 20 minutes, until the garlic looks toasted. Remove from the oven and use a slotted spoon to remove the garlic cloves from the dish and discard. Reduce the oven temperature to 250°F.

Add the peppers to the baking dish in a single layer. Slightly overlapping is fine. Transfer the vessel back into the oven and roast for 1 hour.

Remove the baking dish from the oven and reset to broil. Be sure the oven rack is about 6 inches from the heating element. Carefully transfer the skillet to the oven and broil the peppers until they are barely charred, about 2 to 3 minutes.

Remove the peppers from the oven and serve with crusty bread.

"Mariscos: shellfish eaten in the cafés while drinking beer before or after bullfights."

—*DEATH IN THE AFTERNOON*, GLOSSARY

ALMEJAS CON CHORIZO

Clams with Sausage

TOTAL TIME: 20 minutes
SERVES: 3 to 4 as a tapa or an appetizer

Across ocean-focused areas of Spain, one finds many dishes in which clams are the star. Whether it's called *almejas a la Española*, *almejas a la marinera*, or *almejas en salsa verde*, they're all essentially the same dish, often flavored with cured meat, tomatoes, garlic, white wine, and parsley. Here, we cut to the chase and feature the sausage as the strongest partner for the clam.

- 2 tablespoons vegetable oil
- 3 tablespoons minced red onion
- 3 tablespoons diced Spanish chorizo sausage
- 2 cloves garlic, minced
- 3 tablespoons diced tomato
- ¼ cup lager beer
- ½ teaspoon kosher salt
- 10 middle neck clams
- 2 tablespoons unsalted butter, cold
- 2 tablespoons minced parsley
- Microgreens, for garnish
- Toast points, for serving

Add oil to a wide-bottomed pan over medium heat. When the oil begins to shimmer, add the onion and sauté until the onion is translucent, about 3 to 4 minutes. Add the sausage and continue to sauté until the sausage begins to brown, an additional 3 to 4 minutes. Stir in the garlic and sauté until the garlic is fragrant, about 1 minute.

Stir in the tomatoes, ¼ cup of water, the beer, and salt and bring the mixture to a simmer. Nestle the clams into the mixture, reduce the heat to low, and cover for 7 minutes. While the clams steam, shake the pan a few times to distribute the broth among them. Uncover, add the butter and parsley, and continue to stir until the butter melts.

To finish: Plate the clams in a shallow bowl and pour the sauce over them. Garnish with microgreens and serve with toast points for dipping in the sauce.

"At Valencia too, when it is hottest, you can eat down at the beach for a peseta or two pesetas at one of the eating pavilions where they will serve you beer and shrimps and a paella of rice, tomato, sweet peppers, saffron and good seafood . . . all cooked together in a saffron-colored mound."

—*Death in the Afternoon*

ARRÓZ DEL SENYORET CON SALMONETE
Naked Seafood and Fish Rice

TOTAL TIME: 1 hour, 15 minutes
SERVES: 3 to 4 as an entrée

Let's be frank . . . Manually dismembering sea creatures can be a dining challenge. *Arróz del senyoret*, or "gentlemen's rice," is the clean-handed solution. Cooks in Valencia (or Barcelona or Alicante, depending on the teller of the tale) heeded the centuries-old cry for civility and created the perfect response. Also known as *parellada rice*, or "rich man's rice," this dish diverts shells and bones to the preparation of excellent stock, so diners may fully enjoy their meal with a simple spoon. Without any need for wet wipes.

FISH STOCK (IF USING)

1 pound fish frames (bones, heads, and fins; ask at the fish counter)

Shrimp shells from the rice preparation (below)

1 onion, diced

2 scallions, halved

3 sprigs fresh parsley

1 pinch saffron

TO MAKE THE FISH STOCK, IF USING: Add all the fish stock ingredients to a pot filled with 4 cups of water over medium-high heat and bring to a simmer. Reduce the heat to medium-low and maintain a simmer for 30 minutes. Skim and discard any scum from the surface when necessary. Remove from the heat and strain the stock through cheesecloth, a nut-milk bag, or a fine-mesh strainer. Set the stock aside and discard the solids.

RICE

6 ounces boneless red mullet or rockfish fillet

4 ounces shell-on shrimp, shells divided from meat and reserved

2 tablespoons soy sauce

1 lemon, for juice and zest, divided

4 tablespoons extra-virgin olive oil, divided

1½ teaspoons kosher salt, divided

1 medium tomato, halved, stemmed, grated, and skin discarded

3 cloves garlic, minced

3 tablespoons cognac or other brandy

1 cup Spanish rice, such as *bomba* or *calasparra*

3 cups Fish Stock (see page 114) or 3 cups water, plus 1 tablespoon Thai fish sauce or 1½ cups water, plus 1½ cups clam juice

2 ounces canned *calamarcitos* (tiny squid) or squid rings

TO MAKE THE RICE: In a mixing bowl, evenly coat the fish fillets and shrimp with 1 tablespoon of soy sauce, the juice of ½ of a lemon, 2 tablespoons of olive oil, and ½ teaspoon of salt. Set aside for 30 minutes before continuing the process.

Preheat the oven to 350°F.

Add the remaining 2 tablespoons of olive oil to a *paellera* or large skillet over medium-high heat. When the oil begins to shimmer, add the tomato, garlic, brandy, the remaining 1 teaspoon of salt, and the 1 remaining tablespoon of soy sauce and sauté for 5 minutes, until the liquid has reduced by half. Add the rice and continue to sauté until the rice emits a nutty aroma, about 1 minute.

Carefully pour in 3 cups of fish stock (or an alternative) and stir just once to combine. Increase the heat to high and bring the liquid to a boil. Remove from the heat and transfer the pan to the oven and braise for 15 minutes. Carefully remove the pan from the oven and set the fish fillet, shrimp, and *calamarcitos* or squid rings atop the rice and return to the oven and roast for an additional 10 minutes.

Remove the pan from the oven. Garnish with lemon zest and squeeze the other ½ of lemon juice across the top before serving hot.

CHAPTER 13

THE LAND

A Visit to Central Market

"It was a clean, well-run market and there was plenty to buy but many of the shoppers were bitter about the prices, especially of the fish and meat."

—*The Dangerous Summer*

We ate like beachside royalty and swam like savages in the Mediterranean the day before and paid the price of sleeping the best we have in a while. Today was a day for dry land. Hemingway saw Valencia as a place where the land met the sea with the kind of negotiated peace forged over centuries. In *For Whom the Bell Tolls*, Pilar reminisces on the oxen here hauling fishing boats to the shore, their strength and patience as much a part of the day's work as the haul of the nets. Valencia is the point where effort meets reward, where the sea's gifts are equaled by a harvest from the soil.

The Central Market stands at the heart of it all, a symbol of this equality in which Hemingway marveled. Its vaulted ceilings soared, a temple to what is good, built not to a god but to the honest work of the farmers and the fishers. Art Deco–stained glass catches the sun's new rays in patterns of greens, oranges, and reds, mirroring the produce it housed. It is a place of plenty, even in this shoulder season, when abundance comes not from the calendar but from the diligence of the people who worked the land.

We step farther inside, and the enormity of it takes a moment to sink in. Rows upon rows of vendors, each offering something fresh, something local, something alive with color and vitality. As we amble through, the air changes its mind every ten feet or so. First the aromatic tang of citrus, second the loamy depth of tubers, then the briny whiff of the sea. This was the kind of place Hemingway lingered, following the tales of Valencia not in words but in the senses, the shades of its harvest.

There are stalls selling hot snacks to draw the hunger and stalls offering cold samples that hint at the promise of what they could become at your stove. Sellers stand behind piles of artichokes and persimmons, their hands leathery but quick, moving and rebalancing fruit pyramids with the precision of those who've spent a lifetime with the land. The market is pristine. Even the tiled floors gleam, as though Valencia takes as much pride in the display as in the food itself. At a stand selling take-home paellas, the man presented perfect pans of perfect rice with perfect accouterments that looked like paintings and surely tasted of art.

Around one corner a busy bar caught our eye, not a mere counter for hurried coffee, but something of an operation, altogether different; we are intrigued and grab a seat. Seated next to us are Deana and Fernando, a kindly older couple and retired, or so it seems. Like role models we didn't know we needed, they spend their mornings wandering this market a short walk from home to see, feel, and smell what they might want to cook tonight. Then they sit at this same corner of the bar and have a glass of wine, "something as healthy and normal as food," followed by whatever the chef has on the daily chalkboard. That is the way to live. To us, they are Spain atop two barstools.

Fernando remarks that not everyone has a celebrity chef to cook them breakfast and Deana suggests we help keep their little secret. We assure them it is safe with us. The chef behind it has some stars from that French tire company and you'd hardly guess it from this bar, where the neighborhood

comes to break a fast. It is this way in Spain, where duly acclaimed chefs seldom wear such honors on their sleeves. *Pundonor*, ladies and gentlemen, it visits us again.

The chef's fame doesn't carry weight here, his ingredients do. The menu is filled with the Central Market's greatest hits, a celebration of Valencia in all its shapes. Everything he cooks comes from these vendors and he returns their effort with dishes that tell the story. At times that story is a creative retelling of the original. Some of today's specials seem altogether un-Spanish, Asian to be exact. Maybe the chef heard rumor of our visit and leans into the legend of Hemingway as a spy across the Pacific, but he likely just loves to cook delicious food.

We indulge the tongue-in-cheek conspiracy and first order the *Berenjenas con Soja y Miso* (page 119), eggplant braised in miso and soy sauce. Its charred skin smoky and soft, the butter-like insides barely held together by it, swimming in umami, an almost sweet bath. Despite the undeniably Japanese profile, this plate eats naturally here. The same goes for the *Albóndigas al Curry Rojo* (page 120), meatballs in red curry, that followed. Smooth, nutty, and bright without that expected meatball heft. A nod to a modern trend of Thai infusions, yet grounded in spices that feel as though they'd always belonged here. Not spicy though; Spain just does not do spice.

By the time we wipe our grins of remnants of Phuket, it is late morning, just in time to engage in a rather Valencian ritual, *el esmorzaret*. To be sure, it is hangover food. This meal wedged between breakfast and lunch was more innocently born of the need to feed farmers who arose with the sun, got a little sustenance before hitting the fields, but were then famished by the time the first of their shifts came to a close. It had to be big and it had to be good. We do not move from our stools, not because we've eaten too much or drank this early in the day, but because we want to see what this place did with *esmorzaret*.

Esmorzaret across Valencia became synonymous with sandwiches, a Hemingway staple. Quotations abound, but suffice it to say, in between locations or in between scenes, fictional or not, or in the case of *For Whom the Bell Tolls*, every time Robert Jordan and crew were not eating stew, they were stuffing things between bread. It is the *esmorzaret* that speaks loudest to the intersection of true *Valenciano* and Don Ernesto. This was food for people who work, with big appetites, and with grit, and he would applaud.

The usual places across this city for *esmorzaret* offer large, crusty rolls and a laundry list of fillings from roasts and omelets to cheeses and cold cuts, fresh vegetables and sundry fried seafood. Here, the bar's version came refined, yet honest. On offer were the classics and, by the looks of other diners' smiles, exquisite versions of pork loin and Manchego, crispy calamari, tuna and tomato, and our choice, *Bocadillo de Morcilla y Revueltos* (page 122), blood sausage, scrambled egg, and pickled green peppers. The balance of mineral, creamy, and acidic is stupendous.

We round off the *esmorzaret* like any good Valencian, with a *Cremaet* (page 123), burnt rum coffee. The cinnamon and citrus tones and an ample addition of sugar take the mind away from the rum part of the drink, but not for long. Hemingway would have drained it in a single pull and gone back for another. We play the farmer in this case and resign the post after just one, into the sun but without the hard labor.

We leave the market with the sense that Valencia has opened itself to us in layers. The land and the sea don't just meet here, they wed, work together, thrive together. The farmers and fishers, the chefs and market vendors, the oxen and the boats, all move in the same rhythm, a rhythm Hemingway admired and one we were beginning to understand.

"Most land is owned by those who farm it. Originally the land was owned by the state and by living on it and declaring the intent of improving it, a man could obtain a title to a hundred and fifty hectares."

—*For Whom the Bell Tolls*

BERENJENAS CON SOJA Y MISO
Eggplant with Soy and Miso

TOTAL TIME: 1 hour, 10 minutes
SERVES: 3 to 4 as a tapa or an appetizer, 1 to 2 as a side dish

Spain is having a bit of an affair with Japanese cuisine. As expected in the cities, sushi bars and noodle joints abound. But traditional bars nod to Japan on the usual menu as well. Pot-stickers, teriyaki chicken, and *tataki* tuna have begun to be served as tapas alongside *croquetas* and *jamón*. This dish is a hybrid of sorts, where eggplant is a Spanish stalwart and soy and miso are straight out of Tokyo.

1 globe eggplant, top and bottom edges removed and cut into 2-inch rounds

1 tablespoon kosher salt

2 tablespoons extra-virgin olive oil

3 tablespoons white miso paste

3 tablespoons light soy sauce

2 tablespoons mirin

1 tablespoon sugar

Crusty bread or rice, for serving

Coat the eggplant flesh with the salt and set aside on paper towels for 30 minutes. Rinse and dry. Use a small knife to cut a cross ½ inch deep into the top and bottom of each segment.

Add the olive oil to a high-sided skillet, brazier, or Dutch oven over medium heat. When the oil begins to shimmer, add the eggplant segments flesh-side down and sear for 2 minutes per flesh side. Remove the eggplant from the skillet and set aside.

Add the miso paste, soy sauce, mirin, sugar, and ⅔ cup of water to the same pan and stir until the sugar dissolves. Increase the heat to high and bring the mixture to a boil. Reduce the heat to low, nestle the eggplant into the liquid, cover, and simmer for 10 minutes.

Uncover, flip the eggplant segments, cover, and continue to simmer for 10 to 15 minutes, until the eggplant is very soft, but the skin is still intact.

Remove from the heat, spoon ample amounts of the sauce over the eggplant, and serve hot with crusty bread or rice.

"He could smell food now in the cave, the smell of oil and of onions and of meat frying and his stomach moved with hunger inside of him."

—For Whom the Bell Tolls

ALBÓNDIGAS AL CURRY ROJO

Meatballs in Red Curry

TOTAL TIME: 1 hour, 30 minutes
SERVES: 8 to 10 as a tapa or an appetizer

Spanish chefs have begun incorporating Japanese flavor profiles into traditional fare, and Thai flavors are now not far behind. Ingredients like coconut milk, ginger, and chiles are finding their way into soups and sauces across Spain. This dish takes classic Spanish meatballs and douses them in a taste of Southeast Asia, and the result is a natural pairing.

MEATBALLS (MAKES ABOUT 20)

1 pound ground beef, pork, or a mixture of both

½ onion, grated and squeezed of liquid

2 cloves garlic, minced

1 egg

2 tablespoons milk

3 slices stale white bread, torn into small pieces

1 teaspoon kosher salt

½ teaspoon freshly ground black pepper

½ cup fresh basil, coarsely chopped, divided

RED CURRY SAUCE

3 tablespoons extra-virgin olive oil

1 large onion, diced

1 teaspoon kosher salt

3 tablespoons red curry paste

4 cloves garlic, minced

14 ounces coconut milk

2 red bell peppers, roasted, peeled, seeded, and diced

½ cup beef or chicken stock

Crushed peanuts, for garnish

Crusty bread, for serving (optional)

TO MAKE THE MEATBALLS: Preheat the oven to 425°F. In a large mixing bowl, evenly combine all the meatball ingredients, but only ¼ cup of the basil. Have a lightly greased baking sheet ready. Form the mixture into ping-pong-size balls and place on the baking sheet. Roast the meatballs in the oven for 25 minutes. Start the sauce while they roast. Remove the partially cooked meatballs from the oven, cover with foil and set aside.

TO MAKE THE RED CURRY SAUCE: Heat the olive oil in a Dutch oven over medium-high heat. When the oil begins to shimmer, add the onions and sauté until translucent, about 8 to 10 minutes. Add the salt, curry paste, and garlic and continue to sauté until the garlic is highly aromatic, about 1 minute. Add the coconut milk, bell peppers, and stock and bring to a boil over high heat. Reduce the heat to low and simmer for 10 minutes.

Using either an immersion blender inside the pot or carefully transferring the contents to a blender for a moment, purée the sauce. Submerge the reserved meatballs into the sauce, place a lid on the pot, and continue simmering for 1 hour. Occasionally spoon sauce over any exposed meatballs.

Remove from the heat and transfer the meatballs from the sauce to a serving bowl and pour the sauce over the top. Garnish with crushed peanuts and the remaining basil. Serve alongside crusty bread or just some toothpicks for grabbing.

As we continue our relatively innocent game of runs and sets, Fracassi brings us ruby red *piquillo* peppers, stuffed full of crayfish and minced beef, yet another cut of the bull, a creamy nod to Valencia's land and sea. *Pimientos Rellenos* (page 127) atop bread. They sit on the plate like the filed-down tips of a bull's horns, a quiet wink to tradition, or maybe to Hemingway's grudging acknowledgment of change. When he came back to Spain in the fifties, he found bull's horns dulled a notch, a concession to time or politics, and it didn't sit right with him. The bulls had been softened, but the fight was still there if one looked hard enough.

The rice dish arrived soon after what amounted to the great version of a stuffed pepper. But the *arróz*, it was a spectacular presentation, very much carnal, satisfying and in its round pan a shapely ode to the Valencian bullring, sword-work on full display. We sip beer as would be appropriate in the stands and ate slowly, savoring the cuts, the flavors, the memory of the bull. There was something about this rice, the way it carried the weight of the beef, unlike some chicken and rabbit or seafood. It would not surprise that a dish like this in a town like this with such depth would inspire one to write about bulls and rings and swords.

We say a hearty *arrivedérci* to Fracassi and thank the chef. Outside, the night air is cool, and the city hums with life. Valencia didn't *olé* like Madrid or dance like Sevilla, still it buzzed, steady and true. We walk back across the old river now dressed as a park toward the hotel with the bar for a front desk and have a nightcap. Tomorrow, Pamplona.

"If there was no war I would go with Eladio to get crayfish from that stream back there by the fascist post. One time we got four dozen from that stream in a day."

—For Whom the Bell Tolls

PIMIENTOS RELLENOS
Stuffed Roasted Peppers

TOTAL TIME: 35 minutes
SERVES: 6 to 8 as a tapa or an appetizer

The *piquillo* is the most popular pepper in Spain. When this transplanted chile from the Americas flourished in Navarra, its diminutive size was ideal for tapas, as if the fates saw it fit. The roasted pepper stuffed with meats, cheeses, or seafood is the perfect two-bite snack. Possibilities abound, but this surf-and-turf treatment from Valencia balances the sweetness of the pepper perfectly.

2 tablespoons extra-virgin olive oil, plus more for drizzling

8 ounces ground beef

1 teaspoon kosher salt, divided

½ teaspoon freshly ground black pepper

2 cloves garlic, minced

8 canned or jarred *piquillo* peppers

¼ cup cream cheese, room temperature

2 tablespoons mayonnaise

1 egg yolk

2 tablespoons chopped parsley

8 ounces cooked crayfish tails, peeled

8 slices baguette

Preheat the oven to 375°F.

Add the olive oil to a skillet over medium-high heat. When the oil begins to shimmer, add the beef, ½ teaspoon of the salt, the pepper, and garlic and sauté for 4 to 5 minutes, until the beef is well browned. Remove from the skillet and drain.

Place the *piquillo* peppers on a plate and pat dry with paper towels. In a mixing bowl, whisk together the cream cheese, mayonnaise, egg yolk, parsley, and the remaining ½ teaspoon of salt. Fold in the crabmeat and cooked beef. Using a small spoon, fill each pepper to the top with the beef-and-crab mixture and place on a greased baking sheet. Transfer to the oven and roast for 15 minutes. For the last 5 minutes of roasting, add the baguette slices to toast.

Remove the stuffed peppers and toast from the oven. Place the peppers atop the toast and, optionally, secure with a toothpick. Drizzle with olive oil and serve hot.

"There was no wind, and, outside now of the warm air of the cave, heavy with smoke of both tobacco and charcoal, with the odor of cooked rice and meat."

—*For Whom the Bell Tolls*

ARRÓZ DE VACA MADURADA

Dry-Aged Beef Rice

TOTAL TIME: 1 hour
SERVES: 3 to 4 as an entrée

During our time at Bar Cremaet, our server, Maicol Fracassi, though already drawn in and excited by our game of gin rummy, was also intrigued by the Hemingway project and had read many of his works in Italian. He felt a special connection to *A Farewell to Arms*, given his Italian heritage. He introduced us to Chef Raphael Jean-Louis Pallenhoff Mendez, of French and Spanish descent, also a reader. The duo was honored when we then suggested adding the bar's recipe to the book. Not for the publicity, but for the association with Hemingway. Below is our adaptation of Chef Raphael's *arróz de vaca madurada*.

6-ounce whole piece of boneless, dry-aged *picaña* beef

1½ teaspoons kosher salt, divided

8 ounces boneless, dry-aged *picaña* beef, cut into ½-inch dice

3 tablespoons extra-virgin olive oil, divided

2 teaspoons smoked paprika

3 cups chicken stock

1 pinch saffron

1 medium tomato, halved, stemmed, grated, and skin discarded

2 cloves garlic, minced

1 cup uncooked Spanish round rice, such as *bomba* or *calasparra*

1 sprig fresh rosemary

Season the 6-ounce piece of whole *picaña* with ½ teaspoon of salt and set aside. In a mixing bowl, coat the diced beef with 1 tablespoon of olive oil, ½ teaspoon salt, and 1 teaspoon of paprika. In a heat-proof dish on the stove or in the microwave, heat the stock and saffron for 3 minutes. Set the marinating meat and stock aside for 30 minutes.

Add the remaining 2 tablespoons of olive oil to a *paellera* or wide skillet over medium heat. When the oil shimmers, add the marinated beef and sauté for 4 to 5 minutes, until well browned.

Add the tomato, garlic, and remaining ½ teaspoon of salt to the pan and sauté for 3 minutes. Add the rice and continue to sauté until the rice emits a nutty aroma, about 1 minute. Carefully pour in the saffron-infused stock and stir just once to combine evenly.

Place the rosemary sprig across the top, increase the heat to high, and bring the liquid to a boil. Reduce the heat to medium-high and maintain a strong simmer for 10 minutes. Reduce the heat to medium-low and simmer for an additional 10 to 15 minutes, until the rice has fully absorbed the liquid and is fully cooked. If the rice needs further cooking, but has already absorbed all the liquid, add water ¼ cup at a time and simmer until complete.

While the rice is cooking, grill or sauté the seasoned whole *picaña* to rare or medium-rare, then let it rest while the rice finishes cooking. Slice the meat into ¼-inch tiles across the grain. Remove the rosemary from the rice and lay the tiles of seared *picaña* across the top. Serve hot and hand each guest a spoon and eat directly from the pan.

Vaca Premium 5 Semanas
Vaca Premium 5 Semanas
Vaca Premium 4 Semanas
Vaca Premium 5 Semanas
Vaca Premium 4 Semanas
Vaca Premium 5 Semanas
Vaca Premium 4 Semanas
Vaca Premium 6 Semanas
Vaca Premium 6 Semanas

CHAPTER 15

MORNING WALK

The Bread of War

"Or would you rather smell frying bacon in the morning when you are hungry? Or coffee in the morning? Or a Jonathan apple as you bit into it? Or a cider mill in the grinding, or bread fresh from the oven?"

—For Whom the Bell Tolls

Valencia is a city that knew conflict and bore it in its bones. It was a Republican capital during the Spanish Civil War, a stronghold of the loyalists. Franco never took it in battle. The city fell only when the war ended, a last defiant flame snuffed out by inevitability. Hemingway followed the bulls here before the war and reported from here during it, even enjoyed the odd wartime "get away," if you could call it that, with fellow reporter, lover, and eventual spouse, Martha Gellhorn, between reportings. The city was full of diplomats and spies, artists and intellectuals, politicians and journalists. Hemingway's idea of a good time. The memories rose through his writing, the beauty, the beach, the revelry, the heartbreak.

Just as Valencia was a visage of refuge on the pages of *For Whom the Bell Tolls*, bread also becomes a character. It fed fighters across the front and in the cities, simple, undeniable sustenance in the face of the unknown and of brutality. Bread was survival, solace even, but it was also camaraderie, a small rebellion against hunger and despair. It sopped up stew, carried meat and cheese, embraced flaky fish, and was dunked when staleness set in. Valencia is known for its bread.

We walk the morning neighborhoods of Ciutat Vella and l'Eixample, the middle of town, where the lanes narrow and twist, round a corner, then straighten to a grid. If you know where to look, the streets still carry the weight of war, "the great crime against anything good in the world." We wander through courtyards sitting above the old air-raid shelters that protected a population under bombs, past hundreds of stone buildings built anew since the war and followed the paths and archway memorials of countless injured, and worse. It is not the thought of war that brings the hunger, but food would help to break the gloom.

To pay homage, we return to the central market where refinement meets earth. We are a little late in the day to see our amigos Deana and Fernando, with their morning glass of wine, but in their spirit, we order a chef's specialty, *Coca de Berenjena y Tomate* (page 132), thin and crisp and rich with the land. Creamy eggplant, roasted tomatoes, and fresh spinach layered onto dough that crackles and sighs under the bite. It is Valencian bread at its best, light, delicate, yet sturdy enough to carry the weight of its load. A reminder that food can be both grounded and lifted, a reflection of a city both scarred and beautiful.

Outside the market, the alleyways once again call us deep. We look for *esmorzaret*, overindulgent and oversized, meant to feed a worker in between bouts of labor. So, we watch for a local crowd that tells us by its size the quality that lives inside. From the surrounding compatriots, there is one clear favorite here, *El Chivito* (page 135), which means "little goat" another unwitting and filling character in *For Whom the Bell Tolls*. The sandwich is not of goat but of pork loin and

melted cheese, layered with fried egg, bacon, and tomatoes. It's from Uruguay, but Valencia embraces it as its own. Robert Jordan would envy the proportions and the cheese which isn't "too goaty."

There is room for one more close stop before we depart, and for this we amble just outside the old city, past the once-battered government square to a bakery where another long morning queue vies for Valencia's finest. Forn de San Pablo draws the neighborhood for coffee and *empanadillas*, but their sandwiches also look fetching. As we near the front of the line, the pressure mounts to select wisely from the vaguely labeled treats. We spy the *Empanadilla de Atún* (page 136), a hand pie of fish and peppers. Robert Jordan's Valencian memory. His bites were on the beach, but our time is short. We add icy *Horchata* (page 133) to wash it down.

We find a seat out in the wilds of the Valencia workday, a park bench on which to enjoy a bit of Hemingway in a paper bag. The *empanadilla*'s crust is flaky and golden, the filling of tuna and green peppers warm and rich. The horchata, that expected cool hit of the milk of a tiger nut, sweet as the day is long, chilled as the darkest of night. As we look back at the line outside the bakery and consider a snack for the journey to Pamplona, the fates were with us. A small piece of Valencia along for the ride.

The line has vanished along with most of the *empanadillas*. What remains is a simple sandwich, a *bocadillo de fiambre*. This one is austere, almost stark, nothing like the *esmorzaret*. Bread, tomato smear, and cured meat, nothing more. This is fitting, the way it brought things full circle. Hemingway appreciated the double meaning, "*fiambre* . . . the Spanish slang word for corpse, the same used on menus for cold meat." Bread and death, life and sacrifice, all bound together in some parchment. It's time to start the drive to Pamplona and the festival.

"He crossed the stream, picked a double handful, washed the muddy roots clean in the current and then sat down again beside his pack and ate the clean, cool green leaves and the crisp, peppery-tasting stalks."

—For Whom the Bell Tolls

COCA DE BERENJENA Y TOMATE

Tomato and Eggplant Flatbread

TOTAL TIME: 2 hours
SERVES: 6 to 8 as a tapa or an appetizer, 3 to 4 as an entrée

Whether *coca* bread is Valencian or Catalonian is up for debate, but one thing is for sure, it's a cousin of pizza and/or Northern African flatbreads. Uniquely in Spain, one is likely to see sweet as well as savory treatments, and seldom do they employ cheese. This example is quintessential *coca*, fruits of the earth in various textures.

DOUGH

½ tablespoon kosher salt

1 teaspoon sugar

2 tablespoons extra-virgin olive oil, divided

½ tablespoon rapid-rise yeast

2 cups all-purpose flour, plus more for dusting

TOPPING

One 14-ounce can petite diced tomatoes

1 globe eggplant, roasted and skin discarded

1 teaspoon kosher salt

8 ounces baby spinach, coarsely chopped

½ cup sliced sun-dried tomatoes

2 tablespoons pine nuts, roasted

TO MAKE THE DOUGH: In a small mixing bowl, stir together 1 cup of water, ½ tablespoon salt, the sugar, and 1 tablespoon of olive oil until the salt and sugar dissolve. In a large mixing bowl or the bowl of a stand mixer, whisk together the yeast and flour. With clean hands or low speed with a dough hook in the stand mixer, slowly incorporate the liquid until a single mass of dough forms. Whether by hand or mixer, knead the dough for 5 minutes.

On a lightly floured work surface, knead and form the dough into a smooth ball and transfer to a large bowl greased with olive oil. Cover with plastic wrap or a clean dish towel and allow the dough to proof for 1 hour at room temperature. It should double in size.

Preheat the oven to 400°F.

Remove the dough to a lightly floured work surface and divide into 4 equal portions. Form each portion into a ball, dust with flour, cover, and let rest for 30 minutes.

Roll each ball into a disk about ¼ inch thick and transfer the disks to a flour-dusted baking sheet or two. Brush the tops with olive oil, then use a fork to prick the surface all over. Transfer the pans to the oven and bake for 15 to 20 minutes, until golden brown.

Remove the *cocas* from the oven, top with the diced tomatoes, without too much of the juices, strands of roasted eggplant, then sprinkle with salt. Finish with the spinach, sun-dried tomatoes, and pine nuts. Serve uncut as an entrée or sliced as a tapa.

"It should have the smell of burnt powder and the smoke and the flash and the noise of the traca going off through the green leaves of the trees and it should have the taste of horchata, ice-cold horchata, and the new-washed streets in the sun, and the melons and beads of cool on the outside of the pitchers of beer . . ."

—*Death in the Afternoon*

HORCHATA

Chilled Tiger-Nut Milk

TOTAL TIME: Overnight, plus 10 minutes, plus 1 hour to chill
SERVES: 4 to 6

Horchata in Spain is *horchata de chufa*, or tiger-nut milk, and is not to be confused with *horchata de arróz*, which is Mexican and made of rice. The drink is originally Northern African and meant to be cooling in hot climates. These days, it's common to see variants at places known for the good stuff, and the frozen, frappé-like version is *hot*.

8 ounces dry tiger nuts

1 tablespoon sugar

1 lemon, zested

½ teaspoon ground cinnamon

In a large bowl, cover the tiger nuts with 1 inch of water and soak in the refrigerator overnight.

Remove any loose debris or shells and drain the nuts. In the bowl of a blender, purée the nuts and 2 cups of water until a hummus-like paste forms. Add 2 more cups of water, the sugar, lemon zest to taste, and cinnamon to the bowl and purée until smooth.

Strain the purée through cheesecloth or a nut-milk bag into a pitcher or other container. Be sure to squeeze the straining cloth of as much liquid as possible. Discard the solids. Refrigerate or freeze the horchata for at least 1 hour before stirring, pouring, and enjoying cold. If one chooses the freezer, the result is similar to a frappé.

"The snow was going fast and they were eating breakfast. There were two big sandwiches of meat and the goaty cheese apiece, and Robert Jordan had cut thick slices of onion."

—*For Whom the Bell Tolls*

EL CHIVITO
Pork, Bacon, and Egg Sandwich

TOTAL TIME: 20 minutes
SERVES: 4 as an entrée

This sandwich, the "little goat," originally from Uruguay, is multilayered and hearty. It gained popularity in Valencia through cultural exchange and immigration, though it also fit into an existing fondness for hefty and diverse *bocadillos* one might enjoy during the *esmorzaret*, the midmorning refueling. The main meat layer can be beef, pork, even chicken, but never goat.

4 ciabatta or other sandwich rolls, split top and bottom

4 to 6 tablespoons mayonnaise

1 large tomato, cut into 8 slices

4 boneless pork chops, pounded thin and sautéed with salt and pepper

8 slices aged goat cheese

8 slices lettuce

8 slices cooked bacon

4 fried eggs, cooked over-easy with salt and pepper

Preheat the oven to 400°F. Place halves of the rolls on a baking sheet, open-face up. Spread the surfaces with mayonnaise. On the bottom halves, place 2 tomato slices each, followed by 1 cooked pork cutlet, and a slice of cheese. On the top halves of the rolls, place 1 slice of cheese. Transfer the pan to the oven and toast for 6 to 8 minutes, until the bread is toasty and the cheese has melted. Remove the pan from the oven.

On the bottom halves, above the melted cheese, place the lettuce, bacon, and 1 fried egg. Place the top halves with melted cheese, flipped on top of the bottom halves, closing each sandwich. Serve hot.

"We ate in pavilions on the sand. Pastries made of cooked and shredded fish and red and green peppers and small nuts like grains of rice. Pastries delicate and flaky and the fish of a richness that was incredible."

—*For Whom the Bell Tolls*

EMPANADILLA DE ATÚN

Tuna Turnover

TOTAL TIME: 1 hour, 5 minutes
SERVES: 10 to 12 as a tapa

One typically associates *empanadas* with Argentina, and they are massively popular in the land of the tango. They made their way to South America with the *conquistadors* from Spain and are famously Galician. A Galician *empanada* is a pan-size pastry, filled with sundry ingredients, the most notable of which are tuna and tomato. An *empanadilla*, on the other hand, is the diminutive form, and the smaller they are, the more diverse the possible fillings in one meal.

DOUGH

2¼ cups all-purpose flour, plus more for dusting

8 tablespoons unsalted butter, cold, cut into ½-inch cubes

½ teaspoon salt

1 large egg

FILLING

2 tablespoons extra-virgin olive oil

1 large red bell pepper, cored and diced

1 large green bell pepper, cored and diced

1 large onion, diced

2 cloves garlic, minced

½ teaspoon kosher salt

¼ teaspoon freshly ground black pepper

Two 4-ounce cans solid white tuna in olive oil, drained

TO START THE DOUGH: Add the flour, butter, and salt to the bowl of a food processor. Pulse the mixture until a course meal begins to form, about three to five 1-second pulses. In a small bowl, whisk 1 cup of ice-cold water with the egg. Add the egg mixture into the bowl 1 tablespoon at a time and pulse between tablespoons until clumps of moistened dough form.

Remove clumpy dough from the bowl onto a work surface and form into 2 smooth balls. Wrap the balls individually in plastic wrap and refrigerate for at least 30 minutes.

TO MAKE THE FILLING: Add the olive oil to a skillet over medium heat. When the oil begins to shimmer, add the bell peppers and onion, and sauté for 8 to 10 minutes, until the onion is translucent. Add the garlic, salt, and pepper, and continue to sauté on low for another 10 minutes.

In a large mixing bowl, stir together the tuna-and-onion mixture. Set aside.

TO FINISH THE DOUGH AND BUILD THE *EMPANADILLAS*: Remove the dough from the refrigerator and place on a dusted counter or board. Dust the top of one ball with additional flour and use a rolling pin to form a 9-inch circle about ⅛ inch thick. Cut the dough into 3-inch circles. Set the circles aside under a clean towel. Repeat with the second dough ball, and any extra dough that can be then gathered, rolled, and cut.

Preheat the oven to 375°F. Fill a small bowl with water and set next to the workspace, along with a baking sheet. Place 2 tablespoons of filling atop the center of a dough circle, leaving about ½ inch of free edge. With a wet finger, moisten the edges of the dough and fold over the filling. Use a fork to crimp the edges sealed completely and transfer to the baking sheet. Repeat with all dough circles.

Transfer the baking sheet to the oven and bake for 20 to 25 minutes, until the tops are golden brown.

Remove the *empanadillas* from the oven and serve hot.

Part IV
PAMPLONA

CHAPTER 16

ARRIVAL AND MORNING WALK

Welcome Home

"It was a good morning, there were high white clouds above the mountains. It had rained a little in the night and it was fresh and cool on the plateau, and there was a wonderful view. We all felt good and we felt healthy, and I felt quite friendly to Cohn. You could not be upset about anything on a day like that. That was the last day before the fiesta."

—*The Sun Also Rises*

We arrive late into evening, later than planned and the sun and moon share the autumn sky. Our route from the south and Valencia was longer than once thought, just as Spain was wider than we expected. Distraction played a part with roadside stops to soak in the castle towns, cattle herds, and wheat stalks swaying in the breeze. Hemingway wrote of driving this country and in his postwar treatises remarked on scorched earth and man-made scars, how some of the hillsides were perfect for battle and some perfect for cover.

As we climb the last of the hills into Pamplona, satisfaction sets in. Looking out, we're not merely walking in giant footsteps, but driving in Hemingway's tire treads. "We came into the town on the other side of the plateau, the road slanting up steeply and dustily with shade-trees on both sides, and then leveling out through the new part of town they are building up outside the old walls," Jake Barnes diarized in *The Sun Also Rises*, "then came into the big square by a side street and stopped in front of the Hotel Montoya," his stand-in for long-friend José Quintana's place. For us, it is his more frequented haunt, Gran Hotel La Perla.

We drop our luggage without admiring the Ernest-ness of it all and listen to a louder call, hunger, a primal need. An appropriate stop into a lively bar called Viva San Fermín for a *rabo de toro* sandwich cures the worst of the pang. Hearty and rich and reminiscent of our beautiful plate of oxtail stew in Madrid, succulent hunks of beef wrapped in a long soft roll soaking up the juices. A cold beer sits just right and with batteries back on full it was time to enter Papa's Pamplona, his first Spanish love, thanks to matchmaker Gertrude Stein.

Café Iruña, de facto headquarters of Hemingway and his generation of wayward souls. The main room is palatial with big mirrors and bright chandeliers, and golden walls that echo an allegiance to legend. There is a small bar off to the side, Rincón de Hemingway, they call it, *his corner* at which his bronze-self still stands. We choose terrace seats on the square, now three times the size he knew. *Vermút Casera* (page 145) is in order, as "it was a quiet life," and *vermút* is a quiet drink. This is not the drop of vermouth in a martini or a Manhattan. Spain takes its fortified wine seriously, and the varieties made here would dizzy the American mind.

We meet Dani, a local journalist, a fast friend. He speaks with the rapid ease of someone at home here. He talks of the *San Fermín Txikito*, the little festival commemorating the original feast of the saint. "It's a reunion," he says. "Not just for Pamplona, but for Basques who come from all over to see friends they might not see again until next year." He warns us to rest. "Tomorrow night will be big, bigger than you think." Our tipsy reply, "No bigger than the trout we'll bag in the daytime!" *Vermút* and conviviality wash the day's travel from our bones. We head back to La Perla and sleep well in Hemingway's suite. The ghosts are quiet tonight.

Morning arrives early, up without a hitch. The streets are subdued, waiting, and the air is cool. Like Jake Barnes and his friends, we begin at Bar Txoko on the far side of the square, sip coffee and eat well before moving much. Dani had suggested that we bolster the morning with *Migas de Pastor con Chistorra* (page 143) before the day's adventures. Earthy and satisfying, staled bread, revived with olive oil, fried with bits of bacon and garlic, crowned with a sunny egg and *chistorra*, Hemingway's preferred Navarrese sausage. Simple, lively, reminiscent of Thanksgiving stuffing without the family drama.

We walk through Castillo Square, only slower this time, and appreciate every corner of what became Hemingway's festival domain. Booksellers populate a makeshift readers' market, obscuring the gazebo at the center. A few pilgrims hiking the Camino de Santiago pass by, backpacks tall and full of aspiration. We ask of their path, their yesterday, and their tomorrow and conclude we are on a pilgrimage of our own. Lingering along a twisting spur from the square, we reach the end of this deceptively small town and the old city walls, quiet now, but expectant of an oncoming army of revelers. From the heights, the plain stretches out toward the Pyrenees. The serenity within view inspires the journey of today.

Without a map we feel the city's borders and amble toward the bullring and stop to enjoy a band of Basque troubadours wandering the old town heralding the start of festivities in an ancient way. A few more turns and accordion players and we face the Plaza de Toros, a different kind of city wall. There are no fights today, but we pay homage to the austere memorial to Don Ernesto. He mythologized Pamplona for the world, and this carved stone visage is a fair reminder. For all the blood spilled, this was the arena that sparked one of the great literary obsessions of the twentieth century.

Midmorning brings us back to the square. We pass Café Iruña, pass Txoko, and return to La Perla. In the daylight, we see it clearer, how brazenly close we parked, the car sitting on the walkway in front of the hotel after having crossed the public square. Who does that? We know who. Light falls sharper now on the Hemingway suite, showing what's been changed and what remains. We sit in what they call *his* love seat. The old lines are still there but no doubt reupholstered after the wear of fiestas long gone, after Ava Gardner's posterior made a dent. Plotting our next steps, we lean into the curves and let the moment linger.

We collect the car with the basic effort of walking out the front door and drive toward the mountains ahead of tonight's festivities. Hemingway once advised, "Always do sober what you said you'd do drunk. That will teach you to keep your mouth shut." We seem to recall our midnight brag about catching a big fish. As they beckoned Hemingway, today it is us for whom the trout calls.

"There was a low, dark room with saddles and harness, and hay-forks made of white wood, and clusters of canvas rope-soled shoes and hams and slabs of bacon and white garlics and long sausages hanging from the roof."

—*The Sun Also Rises*

MIGAS DE PASTOR CON CHISTORRA
Breadcrumbs, Fried Egg, and Sausage

TOTAL TIME: 45 minutes
SERVES: 6 to 8 as a tapa, 3 to 4 as an entrée

When we met our friend and Navarrese journalist, Daniel Burgui at Café Iruña, our time seemed short, but the stories long and intriguing. He prepared us for the intense revelry of *San Fermín Txikito*, shared a delicious Basque bit of Magellan history, yes, that Magellan, and talked of a rather provincial upbringing in the countryside surrounding Pamplona. He shared a family memory around *migas de pastor*, shepherd's breadcrumbs:

"*Migas de pastor* is a traditional and very humble recipe that originated in the northern valleys of the Pyrenees but spread across the middle and southern part of Basque Country, thanks to the semi-nomadic shepherds who traveled with the herd during wintertime down from the snowy mountains to the fresh green and flat meadows of the southern part of Navarra.

"After the Civil War and the huge poverty of the postwar times, these kinds of dishes were very popular. The main secret for great Navarrese *migas* is obviously a good-quality bread, homemade, baked in the oven, but stale, from three or four days. The second one is a good *chistorra* from Navarra and Spanish *jamón* diced. The little spoon of olive oil with some garlic mixed with the fat of the [bacon] melted in the same pot will be a perfect smooth and oily bed for the breadcrumbs. The idea is to make the bread live again. The perfect *migas de pastor* texture is like a cake breadcrumb, but salty and topped in the festival of *chistorra* and bacon. Some purists also added lamb fat to make the texture even fattier.

"I clearly remember the autumn Sundays at my grandparents' home eating *migas* from a huge pot in the middle of the table with my little cousins. This was one of our favorite dishes, specially prepared by my grandpa, Nicolás Iguzkiza. He was never a shepherd; he used to work as a road builder for the government of Navarra. But I think these kinds of full-of-energy dishes were also used among these workers to face the cold winds and hard conditions. We as kids truly loved the texture, the softness, and the taste of *migas*, but also eating all together in a shared pot, each one picking their bite with a big spoon. For all the family, that builds a sense of belonging and community."

Continued on the following page is our adaptation of Dani's grandpa's *migas de pastor*.

12 ounces stale bread, torn into 1-inch pieces

3 tablespoons extra-virgin olive oil

8 ounces bacon, diced

1 small tomato, halved, cored, grated, and skin discarded

3 cloves garlic, minced

1 tablespoon smoked paprika

1 teaspoon kosher salt

3 to 4 links Spanish *chistorra*

3 to 4 large eggs

Preheat the oven to 350°F.

In a large colander, lightly sprinkle the bread pieces with water and toss until each piece is barely moist, not soggy. The pieces need to stay intact. Set the colander aside over with a plate.

Add 1 tablespoon of the olive oil to an oven-safe skillet over medium heat. When the oil begins to shimmer, add the bacon and sauté until browned, about 7 to 9 minutes. Add the tomato pulp, garlic, paprika, and ½ teaspoon of salt and continue to sauté until the tomato liquid has evaporated, an additional 5 to 7 minutes.

Add the bread pieces and continue to sauté until the moisture within the bread has evaporated, an additional 7 to 9 minutes. Transfer the skillet to the oven and roast until the bread begins to brown, about 10 to 15 minutes.

In a separate skillet, use the remaining olive oil to brown the sausage and fry the eggs to the desired doneness, sprinkling the tops with the remaining ½ teaspoon of salt. Remove the *migas* from the oven and serve topped with sausage and fried eggs.

"Brett and Mike never got up until noon. We all had a vermouth at the café. It was a quiet life and no one was drunk."

—*The Sun Also Rises*

VERMÚT CASERA
House-Made Fortified Wine

TOTAL TIME: 45 minutes, plus overnight
SERVES: 6 to 8

Vermút in Spain is much more than a drop or two in a martini. It's a whole industry of fortified wines of varying qualities, aging, and ultimate flavor. Like sherry or wine, *vermút* is taken seriously, and may have an afternoon hour dedicated to it, *la hora de vermút*. The drink is joined by salty snacks like olives, cheeses, meats, or canned seafood—the unassuming hero of Spanish gastronomy.

1 cup sugar

1 whole orange zest

1 whole lemon zest

1 cup brandy

1 cup dry sherry

1 whole star anise

4 cloves

1 cinnamon stick

¼ teaspoon green peppercorns

¼ teaspoon coriander seeds

1 sprig fresh rosemary

1 sprig fresh thyme

Two 750-milliliter bottles pinot grigio or other dry white wine, divided

Citrus slices and olives, for garnish

Add the sugar and ⅓ cup of water to a heavy-bottomed pot over medium heat. Constantly stir the sugar as it slowly melts. If the sugar sticks to the sides of the pot, use a wet pastry brush to clean the sides of the pot. When the sugar melts completely, within 8 to 10 minutes, reduce the heat to medium-low. Stir in the orange zest, lemon zest, and brandy. If the caramel seizes, continue to stir patiently until the caramel dissolves and blends into the brandy. Remove from the heat and stir in the sherry, anise, cloves, cinnamon stick, peppercorns, coriander, rosemary, thyme, and 1 cup of wine. Allow the mixture to cool for 1 hour at room temperature. Transfer the mixture to a covered container and refrigerate overnight.

Remove the mixture from the refrigerator and strain through a cheesecloth or a nut-milk bag into a large container. Stir in the remaining white wine and refrigerate for at least 1 hour, until chilled. Serve over ice, garnished with citrus and olives.

CHAPTER 17

THE COUNTRYSIDE

Call of the Mountains

"Then the road came over the crest, flattened out, and went into a forest. It was a forest of cork oaks, and the sun came through the trees in patches, and there were cattle grazing back in the trees. We went through the forest and the road came out and turned along a rise of land, and out ahead of us was a rolling green plain, with dark mountains beyond it. These were not like the brown, heat-baked mountains we had left behind."

—*THE SUN ALSO RISES*

We leave Pamplona midmorning, the sun warm on the square but the air still crisp. The mountains draw us out, their slopes promising cool waters and quiet roads. Hemingway's countryside is our destination, though it is not "trouty" now, it isn't the season, and we don't mind. The currents that feed this earth are still there, and the "great virgin forest of the Irati that was unchanged since the time of the Druids." The river meandering and affirming, the way it was for Jake and Bill in *The Sun Also Rises*, and that was enough.

The road rises gently, cutting through fields and woods, past stone shacks acing the water. The Irati River plays hide-and-seek as we go, a flash of glisten here and there among green trees. Where the river gets thicker, clear and bright, we bare our feet and let the cold water run over them. The leaves whisper with the wind, and the birds call, plotting their next ascent. It smells of pine and soil and the dampness of the riverbank silt.

Farther on, the road narrows and winds through hamlets of white walls and red roofs. Smoke hangs in the air, loose at first but growing tighter, sweet and sharp. We find the source at a small café with a smoking barrel out back. The alderwood burns low, curling clouds around the building. Inside, a chalkboard lists the day's offering, trout from the river farm nearby. As Hemingway would admire, the fish were "beautifully colored and firm and hard from the cold water."

Jake Barnes and Bill Gorton enjoyed the trout fried along with a hearty soup of beans and vegetables. Yet, this place provides a somewhat lighter fare. The *Trucha Ahumada* (page 147) is smoked like Hemingway would stock on Spanish road trips. And those same beans and vegetables meet not in a soup but a salad, *Ensaladilla de Alubias* (page 148). We sit on a perch by the window as the plates arrive, the trout slightly bronzed, and an aura of the alderwood. The salad, cool and cheerful with olive oil, lemon, ham, and herbs, a dish that holds together the river and the land on a single fork.

We linger over the meal, watching the river shine and smoke twist from the chimney rising into the trees. It feels still here, away from the city noise and the square. To honor Jake and Bill and just for laughs, we order a simple roasted chicken to go, if only to once and later gesture with a "drumstick in one hand and the bottle of wine in the other." The roast smells of fire, salt, and Pyrenees air and the crispy bird lasting the drive back to Pamplona would be a miracle.

By midafternoon, we are back behind the wheel and the car cuts through hills and valleys toward taller sharper peaks and France. The Irati slips away behind us. We cross paths with Hemingway's retreat of Burguete, at this hour the hostel is closed up without reason, maybe a siesta, not a soul around. Deeper on the road we meet the monastery at Roncesvalles standing watch like a sentinel over the pass as we turn back to descend toward Pamplona.

Castillo Square awaited our return, no longer warm but ready to heat up with the night's festivities. The festival would begin in earnest, but for now, the mountains and the aroma of alderwood stay with us, quiet and steady, like they were in the beginning. The roast chicken nowhere to be found.

"As I baited up, a trout shot up out of the white water into the falls and was carried down. Before I could finish baiting, another trout jumped at the falls, making the same lovely arc and disappearing into the water that was thundering down."

—*The Sun Also Rises*

TRUCHA AHUMADA

Smoked Trout

TOTAL TIME: 2 hours, 30 minutes
SERVES: 6 to 8 as an entrée

Trout is not the first fish that comes to mind when considering Spanish cooking. But in the Basque Country, particularly in the Pyrenees Mountains, *trucha* is big business. Indeed, without *The Sun Also Rises*, one might not have even guessed that there is a river-fishing culture in Spain. Most of these fish now come from trout farms in the region, but the image of hip waders and flies is a romantic one.

½ cup kosher salt

½ cup brown sugar, packed

1 tablespoon fresh thyme leaves

Four 5- to 7-ounce boneless trout fillets

½ cup alder or oakwood chips

In a mixing bowl, blend together the salt, sugar, and thyme leaves. Coat the flesh side of the trout fillets with the mixture and set uncovered in the refrigerator for 2 hours.

Remove the trout from the refrigerator, rinse off the cure mixture, and dry with paper towels.

Cover the inside of a wok or stovetop smoker with foil. If using a wok, fold loose foil over the rim. Place wood chips in a pile at the middle bottom of the vessel atop the foil. Place a rack above the wood. If using a wok, a round rack works well.

Place the wok or smoker on the stovetop over high heat and cover the vessel. Turn on the extractor fan and open the kitchen windows, so errant smoke can escape. When wisps of smoke begin to come out of the vessel, reduce the heat to medium-low, uncover, and place the trout fillets on the rack. Cover the vessel once again. If using a wok, use the extra foil over the rim to seal the lid to the wok as much as possible.

Smoke the trout for 6 minutes. Turn off the heat and let it sit in the vessel for an additional 6 minutes. Remove the trout fillets from the smoker. Repeat with additional trout.

Serve smoked trout at room temperature or chilled, flaked, with a white bean or other salad.

"The girl brought in a big bowl of hot vegetable soup and the wine."

—*The Sun Also Rises*

ENSALADILLA DE ALUBIAS

White Bean Salad

TOTAL TIME: 10 minutes, plus 1 hour
SERVES: 6 to 8 as a side dish

Of all the vegetables that arrived in Europe during the Colombian Exchange, beans often get a mere honorable mention next to the Spanish darlings of potatoes and peppers. But beans provided a renewable source of protein that didn't involve animals, and this should be enough for top billing, right? Alas, the chickpea from Northern Africa has been around for longer. Spanish bean recipes deserve more screen time.

- 1 tablespoon Dijon mustard
- 3 tablespoons extra-virgin olive oil
- 2 tablespoons freshly squeezed lemon juice
- 1 shallot, minced
- 3 cloves garlic, minced
- 1 tablespoon fresh rosemary leaves
- 3 scallions, thinly sliced
- 1 teaspoon kosher salt
- ½ teaspoon freshly ground black pepper
- Two 14-ounce cans great northern or other small white beans, drained
- 1 cup shredded red cabbage
- 4 ounces cooked green beans, diced
- ½ cup frozen peas, thawed
- 2 ounces Spanish ham or *Jamón Ibérico*, diced (optional)

In a mixing bowl, whisk together the mustard, olive oil, lemon juice, shallot, garlic, rosemary, scallions, salt, and pepper. Fold in the beans, cabbage, green beans, peas, and ham, if using. Refrigerate the salad for at least 1 hour.

Remove the salad from the refrigerator. Stir to redistribute the dressing and serve alongside smoked trout or other main dish.

CHAPTER 18

FIESTA DE SAN FERMÍN

A Very Hemingway Party

"People were coming into the square from all sides, and down the street we heard the pipes and the fifes and the drums coming. They were playing the riau-riau music, the pipes shrill and the drums pounding, and behind them came the men and boys dancing. When the fifers stopped they all crouched down in the street, and when the reed-pipes and the fifes shrilled, and the flat, dry, hollow drums tapped it out again, they all went up in the air dancing. In the crowd you saw only the heads and shoulders of the dancers going up and down."

—*THE SUN ALSO RISES*

We return to Pamplona as the sun begins to set, the autumn light fading over the rooftops. The square hums with life, the smaller *San Fermín Txikito* festival has begun. This is not the San Fermín of international hordes in July, not Don Ernesto's party of lore, the bulls don't run and the mayhem more subdued. Still, it feels more like the Pamplona that first seduced Hemingway, before his words brought the world to its streets. "I've written Pamplona once and for keeps. It is all there as it always was except forty thousand tourists have been added," he once lamented. Tonight, though no bulls, the crowds smaller, and Pamplona's first bishop celebrated without one runner gored, it feels closer to his "goddamnedest wild time."

The square grows ever lively, but we have our own plans first. We walk off the plaza toward the restaurant row of San Nicolás Street, where Restaurante Baserriberri and Chef Iñaki Andradas wait for us. Dinner early by Spanish standards, but the timing is right, the crowd light. The menu is inventive, daring, a tribute to the spirit of the festival, an alternative risk to a mad dash dodging sharp bull horns. We start with a glass of Crianza, full and red, grounding us for the night ahead. The *bOOmVeja* (page 158) arrives first, a playful dish, tender threads of meat on a cream-filled Japanese pancake, served in a shell of a bomb that pours smoke as it's served. It's a show, but also a stunner of lamb, bread, and an explosive, *For Whom the Bell Tolls* on a platter.

Next comes the *ressandwich*, oxtail deep with flavor, shredded and pressed into toast points, touched by a hot-and-sour sauce and inexplicably served atop an ornate stone. Then a hot dog made of local *chistorra* sausage, spiced and bold, whimsically presented in a bull-shaped box. The only bull we see this evening, and cardboard will do just fine. A quail leg, deep-fried like a miniature Southern specialty and paired with a sharp aioli, rounds out the meal. Hemingway loved adventure, and he loved his food, though usually not on the same plate. Baserriberri drives that razor's edge with mastery.

The square is buzzing now as we emerge from San Nicolás, its energy infectious. A band plays under the colonnade, and we're drawn to it. It isn't traditional, it's ska with a Basque edge, trombones, a tuba, and drums pounding out a rhythm that demands movement. Humanity gathers, follows. We're swept into the throng like a parade, dancing as the band leads us along the edges of the square. Rain begins to fall, but the colonnade keeps us all dry, and the music powers through.

Bars along the way tempt the crowd, and some duck in for drinks, wine in disposable cups, cocktail glasses these bars will never see again. We try the same, battling for space

through packed doorways but unwilling to let the band get too far ahead. Fits and starts and failure, but still the music is magnetic, so we stay close. Finally, it may have been Bar Txoko that found us victorious in our hunt for a gin tonic. Who can remember or see signs amid the insanity? The parade continues, the gin and the rain adding a gleam to the cobblestones beneath our feet.

The band turns into a narrow corridor just off the square, a dead end. The space is tight, and the crowd can't all fit. Maybe some three hundred lucky few. Those who remain press close, the music echoing off the walls. Friend groups struggle to take selfies in shoulder-to-shoulder space, and we help snap a shot or two or twenty. And they of us. All part of the dance. It's electric, but hunger eventually pulls us away, slowly. The tapas of the old town beckon, *pintxos* they call them here, and we follow our noses and fellow revelers into the bars lining the path.

The first stop, naturally standing-room only, offers a tight corner perch we use to pause and watch people, take in the flow, the rituals, the practicalities of getting food and drink in this madness. We observe the eventual embrace of long friends as they catch eyes across the packed room, the gentle nudge that alerts someone to let another by, the sung anthems in passing, the thrill when a hungry celebrant finally gets their *pintxo* after battling the masses. This is how salmon must feel, we think, apart from the songs.

As Hemingway taught, "A man can be destroyed but not defeated," we thread through the crowd. The first success at winning our own plate at the bar, the *Mojama con Cebollas Encurtidas* (page 155), salt-cured tuna, "the ham of the sea," topped with pickled red onions. It's briny, sharp, tamed slightly by good olive oil, perfect with another glass of Crianza. At the bar next door, though we're likely daft to leave the safety of the first, painstakingly offers *txangurro*, spider crab crowned with lox and baby eels that Hemingway said "resembled bamboo sprouts slightly crisped at the tips but had a more lubricious texture." A bit eerie, but delicious.

We find Bodegón Sarría next, drawn by the smell of charred mushrooms and zucchini draped in a bright red pepper sauce. It was only ho-hum and warranting of one more Crianza. But, as Hemingway attested, "critics are men who sit and watch a battle from a high place and come down to shoot the survivors." And we're not critics. Another hop down the street, tempura-fried shrimp, crisp and light, and along with the *mojama* and *txangurro*, a collective nod to Hemingway's love of everything aquatic.

Then comes Bar Gaucho, Pamplona's most famous temple of *pintxos*. Though it opened well after Hemingway's time, he would have admired the look, the feel of classic Spanish authenticity, and also the bar's seamless operation, the dishes emerging with military precision on a cramped night like this. Cold *pintxos* on the bar for the taking, hot *pintxos* appearing like clockwork from the tiny but powerful kitchen. We meet Iñaki, the manager here who is more a matador than a barkeep. He leads his crew not of *banderilleros* and *picadors*, but of drink crafters and cooks through flawless passes to a demanding mob, his "domination of the bull." He calls his *pintxos* "the best of Basque cuisine, only tiny." And we agree.

Iñaki has an eel dish of his own to be proud of, but of the adult variety, *Pintxo de Anguila y Tomate* (page 156). This one is a fillet set atop a tomato gel and a sliver of white toasted bread. They serve it with cubes of that same savory tomato gel. Elegant and delicious, and persuasive for those afraid of eel.

Last, the showstopper, the dish that disappears as quickly as it appears on the *pintxo* bar is their *Huevo Trufado* (page 153), the truffled egg. Mrs. Hemingway the second, Pauline Pfeiffer, would have approved of such luxury, and Ernest such an egg. A glass filled with black truffle cream in which a perfectly soft-cooked egg rests, topped with crisp French fries and dust of *jamón*. The flavors are bold, but the execution is surprising and simple.

As we walk back toward the square, the festival is in full swing. The streets are rivers of people, laughter and music spilling from every corner. At the confluence of three alleyways, the crowd swells, a living, breathing thing. We meet three strangers-turned-friends here, likely by stepping on a foot or three: José, Mikel, and yet another Iñaki. They greet us with warmth, embracing us as the only foreigners in sight. Our Spanish is like their English, sparse, but effective. They, like many others in this sea of humanity, are here to reunite with old friends, the ones they see but once each year during the *Txikito*. And now us.

The trio takes us in, guiding us through the mass of revelers. We talk of Hemingway, of Spain, of Basque pride, and of food. Was Don Ernesto a good cook? Could he make paella? Would he add chorizo? The questions are half-serious, half-playful, the kind of banter that flows easily among new amigos. After an hour, they disappear into a crowded bar, but we had our fun. Then, they emerge triumphantly with drinks for us all. As a gesture of true camaraderie, they gift us their traditional blue neckerchiefs, marking us honorary members of their clan. It's a small but meaningful moment, one Hemingway wrote about, a connection forged in the heart of a madcap festival.

The night stretches on, the rain long forgotten, the music and laughter our bosom companions. Eventually, we find ourselves back in the square, watching the lights and merrymakers dance on the wet stones. The festival feels timeless, unhurried, alive in a way that the modern San Fermín cannot be. It is a smaller celebration, yes, but no less significant. A festival unspoiled by spectacle and overflowing with soul. We feel it and Hemingway would be home.

Back at our suite, his suite, we leave the balcony doors open to Estafeta Street for the cool post-rain air, that freshly clean smell that cannot be replaced, and the joyful noise fading over time. If only to keep living it the best we can, but far too burnt to party in earnest into the wee hours. The sounds of this life happening and this breeze are enough, and even Jake Barnes and crew would approve of our calling it a night.

"It was obvious now that it took both Antonio's and Luis Miguel's names to fill a bull ring at the huge price for tickets they were forcing the promoters to ask. If something happened to either one they would smash the whole basket of golden eggs."

—THE DANGEROUS SUMMER

HUEVO TRUFADO

Truffled Egg

TOTAL TIME: 30 to 35 minutes
SERVES: 4 as a tapa

Truffles are a luxury item and one that the Spanish prioritize and keep reasonably priced. Spain is the world's largest producer of black truffles, particularly in Catalonia, and the tonnage that is kept domestically is generously employed throughout the cuisine. Truffles can add a hint of chic to any dish, but they are most commonly used in egg dishes.

TRUFFLED BÉCHAMEL (MAKES ABOUT 2 CUPS)

2 tablespoons unsalted butter

2 tablespoons all-purpose flour

2 cups whole milk, cold

1 teaspoon black truffle paste

½ teaspoon kosher salt

COMPOSITION

2 ounces Spanish ham, *Jamón Ibérico*, or prosciutto, thinly sliced

4 soft-boiled eggs, peeled

4 ounces crispy French fries, hot

TRUFFLE CREAM

1⅓ cups vegetable oil

2 teaspoons black truffle oil

½ cup sheep or cow's milk

1 tablespoon rice vinegar

½ teaspoon kosher salt

TO MAKE THE TRUFFLED BÉCHAMEL: Add the butter to a saucepan over medium heat. As the butter melts, stir in the flour until well combined. Continue stirring for 2 minutes as the mixture bubbles. Switch to a whisk and slowly pour in the milk while continuing to stir. When the mixture comes to a boil, reduce the heat to medium-low, stir in the truffle paste and salt and continue to stir for 2 minutes. Reduce the heat to low. Allow the mixture to simmer while making the ham salt. Extra béchamel may be refrigerated for up to 1 week.

TO MAKE THE FINAL COMPOSITION: Preheat the oven to 400°F. Place the ham slices on a baking sheet lined with parchment paper and transfer to the oven to roast for 5 to 8 minutes. The finished ham should be crispy, but not burnt. Watch carefully. Remove from the oven and set aside to cool for 10 minutes. Place the ham in a food processor and pulse into ham salt.

In 4 glasses or small bowls, add ¼ to ⅓ cup of béchamel to each. Place a soft-boiled egg in each, top with French fries, and dust with ham salt. Instruct diners to mix it all together and enjoy.

"Mike was sitting at a table with several men in their shirt-sleeves, eating from a bowl of tuna fish, chopped onions and vinegar. They were all drinking wine and mopping up the oil and vinegar with pieces of bread."

—*The Sun Also Rises*

MOJAMA CON CEBOLLAS ENCURTIDAS

Salt-Cured Tuna and Pickled Onions

TOTAL TIME: 48 hours, 45 minutes
SERVES: 4 to 6 as a tapa or an appetizer

Tuna fishing in Spain is a major industry and, unsurprisingly, Japan is Spain's biggest customer. Of the fish that remain in Spain, fresh cuts are gaining in popularity, and canned tuna is evergreen. But salt-cured tuna hardly gets a mention. *Mojama* is the ham of the sea, and if it is on a restaurant menu, it's used in much the same way as good *jamón*.

CURED TUNA

1 cup iodized salt

12 ounces sashimi-grade tuna loin

½ cup extra-virgin olive oil

PICKLED RED ONION

1 large red onion, thinly sliced

½ cup distilled white vinegar

½ cup sugar

1 teaspoon kosher salt

ROASTED ALMONDS

4 ounces raw almonds

2 tablespoons extra-virgin olive oil

TO CURE THE TUNA: In a container just large enough to store the whole piece of tuna, pour a bed of salt about ¼ inch thick. Place the tuna atop the salt, then pour more salt on the sides and atop the tuna to cover it completely. Cover the container and transfer it to the refrigerator for 24 hours.

Remove the salted tuna from the refrigerator and rinse off all the salt. Pat dry. Place the tuna on a paper-towel-lined plate and transfer it back to the refrigerator without a cover for 24 hours more.

TO MAKE THE PICKLED RED ONION: Place the onion slices in a heat-proof bowl. In a small pot on the stove, bring the vinegar, ½ cup of water, the sugar, and salt to a boil and ensure that the sugar and salt are dissolved. Pour the mixture over the onions, cover, and set aside for at least 1 hour to cool. Extra pickled onions can be refrigerated for up to 3 weeks.

TO FINISH THE TUNA AND ROAST THE ALMONDS: Preheat the oven to 350°F. Pour ½ cup of olive oil into a small, rimmed baking dish. Cut the tuna into ⅛-inch or thinner slices and place them into the oil within the baking dish. Once all of the tuna slices are in the dish, make sure each is coated with olive oil and then transfer to the refrigerator for 30 minutes.

In a small mixing bowl, toss the almonds with 2 tablespoons olive oil. Transfer to a baking sheet and then to the oven and roast for 10 to 15 minutes, stirring occasionally, until browned without burning.

Remove the tuna from the refrigerator and serve with roasted almonds and topped with a few drained pickled onions.

Ernest: "Eels are excellent. Can't really tell about the wine yet. Care for any eels?"

Bill: "Perhaps a single order. Try the wine. You may like it."

—*The Dangerous Summer*

PINTXO DE ANGUILA Y TOMATE

Eel and Tomato Canapé

TOTAL TIME: 6 hours, plus 15 minutes
SERVES: 3 to 6 as a tapa or an appetizer

We've enjoyed many tapas bars across Spain, but Bar Gaucho in Pamplona is snugly within the best-of-breed category. Not only is the food simultaneously cuisine-defining and defying, but the operation is flawless. Did the food draw the crowd or did the crowd inspire great food and perfect service? We asked Iñaki Ayensa and Carlos Prieto, Bar Gaucho GM and owner, respectively. Their take is that *pintxo* creativity, line efficiency, and the nightly masses grew in sync. And as their popularity blossomed, the dishes became more cutting-edge. Not foams and vapors, but classical techniques brought into a new format. Iñaki leans into Bar Gaucho's mantra of "cuisine, miniaturized." According to him, it's best to have access to the entirety of Spanish cooking and "figure out how to make it tiny and great." The standout dishes were their eel toast and the truffled egg, both unknown to us before that night in Pamplona.

TOMATO ASPIC

1 tablespoon unflavored gelatin granules

2 cups unseasoned tomato juice

½ teaspoon table salt

¼ teaspoon sugar

CANAPÉS

¼ cup pitted black olives

1 cup extra-virgin olive oil

2 slices white bread, crusts removed, toasted and cut into 6 batons

Six ½-inch batons Tomato Aspic (see recipe above)

Two 3½-ounce cans eel fillets in olive oil

1 teaspoon flaky sea salt

TO MAKE THE TOMATO ASPIC: In a small heat-proof bowl, stir 2 tablespoons cold water with the gelatin granules and let it sit for 5 minutes. Stir in ¼ cup of boiling water. Pour the tomato juice and add the salt and sugar into a pot over medium-high heat and bring to a boil. Remove from the heat and stir in the gelatin mixture.

Pour the mixture at ½-inch depth into a shallow silicone mold or silicone ice tray. Transfer to the refrigerator and chill for 4 to 6 hours, until completely solid. Remove from the refrigerator and slice the aspic into six ½-inch-thick batons.

TO BUILD THE CANAPÉS: Blend together the olives and olive oil. On each slice of toast, place 1 baton of tomato aspic, followed by 1 eel fillet, and drizzle with the olive oil mixture and dust with flaky sea salt. Serve.

"Golz knew that once they had passed overhead and on, the bombs would fall, looking like porpoises in the air as they tumbled. And then the ridge tops would spout and roar in jumping clouds and disappear in one great blowing cloud."

—*For Whom the Bell Tolls*

BOOMVEJA! PINTXO DE CORDERO

Shredded Lamb Canapé

TOTAL TIME: 3 hours
SERVES: 6 to 8 as a tapa or an appetizer

Baserriberri restaurant in Pamplona is a circus of food and manager Javier Sánchez is the right host for the job. His hospitality was stellar. Javier was also very comprehensive when talking about the vision of Chef Iñaki Andradas and their approach to local, sustainable, and humanely raised ingredients. It was a fascinating juxtaposition of serious messaging and outlandish presentation. The *bOOmVeja* is a perfect embodiment of our visit and of today's Spanish culinary ethic. Here is our adaptation of Chef Iñaki's prize-winning dish, minus the pyrotechnics.

BRAISED LAMB

1-pound boneless lamb leg or shoulder cut into 1-inch chunks

1½ teaspoon kosher salt, divided

2 tablespoons extra-virgin olive oil, divided

1 star anise

1-inch piece fresh ginger, peeled and minced

¼ cup mirin

1½ cups lamb or beef stock

1 small onion, diced

1 teaspoon smoked paprika

½ cup prepared kimchi

8 teaspoons black or white sesame seeds

PANCAKES (MAKES 8 TO 10)

1¼ cups all-purpose flour

1 teaspoon baking soda

2 eggs

¼ cup sugar

½ teaspoon kosher salt

1 tablespoon honey

¾ cup sheep or cow's milk

Vegetable oil, for frying

TO START THE BRAISED LAMB: Preheat the oven to 300°F. Season the lamb chunks with 1 teaspoon of salt.

Add 1 tablespoon of olive oil to a Dutch oven or other oven-safe pot over medium-high heat. When the oil begins to shimmer, add the lamb. Sear the meat until well browned, 5 to 7 minutes in total. Add the anise, ginger, mirin, and 1 cup of stock and bring to a boil. Remove the pot from the heat, cover, and transfer to the oven and braise for 2½ to 3 hours, until the meat shreds easily using a fork. While the lamb cooks, make the sauce, pancakes, and truffle cream.

Add the remaining 1 tablespoon of olive oil to a skillet over medium heat. When the oil begins to shimmer, add the onion, and the remaining ½ teaspoon of salt and sauté for 6 to 8 minutes, until the onion is translucent. Add the paprika and kimchi and continue to sauté for 2 minutes, until very fragrant. Transfer the mixture to a blender and purée. Add stock 1 tablespoon at a time, until the sauce reaches the consistency of a thick gravy. Set aside.

TO MAKE THE PANCAKES: In a mixing bowl, whisk together the flour and baking soda. In a separate mixing bowl, whisk together the eggs, sugar, salt, honey, and milk. Evenly whisk the wet ingredients into the dry.

Heat a nonstick pan over medium-low heat with a small amount of oil and wipe the excess oil well. Drop 2 tablespoons of batter onto the pan, like a pancake. Cook 2 minutes until small bubbles appear across the surface of the pancake. Flip it over and cook 1 more minute. Remove the pancake from the pan and onto a covered plate. Repeat with the remaining batter.

TRUFFLE CREAM

1⅓ cups vegetable oil

2 teaspoons black truffle oil

½ cup sheep or cow's milk

1 tablespoon rice vinegar

½ teaspoon kosher salt

TO MAKE THE TRUFFLE CREAM: Using an immersion blender, place all the ingredients in a clear round container that just fits the width of the blender (a glass 2-cup liquid measuring cup works well). Hold the blades of the blender flat against the bottom of the container and turn it on. As you observe white gel forming at the bottom of the container, slowly raise the blades straight up, following the growth of the white gel. Once you reach the surface of the emulsion, all should be combined.

TO FINISH THE BRAISED LAMB: Remove the lamb from the oven and strain the meat from the accumulated liquid. In a mixing bowl, shred the meat using 2 forks. Add the kimchi-pepper sauce by the tablespoon until a desired texture is achieved—a bit wetter than a pulled-pork sandwich.

TO PLATE: Place half of the finished pancakes on a platter and top each with 2 tablespoons of truffle cream. Place the remaining pancakes on top of each. Top the pancake sandwich with about 2 tablespoons of lamb mixture. Sprinkle each sandwich with sesame seeds and serve.

CHAPTER 19

MORNING WALK AND A SWIM

The Party's Over

"In the morning it was all over. The fiesta was finished. I woke about nine o'clock, had a bath, dressed, and went down-stairs. The square was empty and there were no people on the streets. A few children were picking up rocket-sticks in the square. The cafés were just opening and the waiters were carrying out the comfortable white wicker chairs and arranging them around the marble-topped tables in the shade of the arcade. They were sweeping the streets and sprinkling them with a hose."

—*THE SUN ALSO RISES*

First light beams through the curtains and doors we left open to the balcony and rouses us from our well-earned sleep. A chill had moved into the room, slowly replacing the bluster of revelers over the wee hours. Now there is silence, no shouts or clinking or songs or even whispers to break the quiet. A few distant screeches of brooms on cobblestone, that's all. We stand on the balcony over Estafeta Street taking it all in. This was Hemingway's favorite perch for the running of the bulls, above the fray. Some say he never ran it. A few of his mended ribs beg to differ.

We hit refresh, shower, toss on clothes and head down the stairs and into the streets, eager to witness the aftermath of *San Fermín Txikito* at ground level. One hundred feet into the square, Café Iruña's terrace and vapors of freshly brewed coffee beckon. After a night like last night, we spy a way to keep our intake simple and even nod to Jake Barnes's hostel out in Burguete. *Tosta con Mantequilla y Mermelada* (page 162), crisp toast, butter, raspberry jam, and a *café con leche*. That hits the spot. Iruña feels relaxed, as if exhaling after the madness of the past eighteen hours or so.

Outside the terrace, the square is immaculate. Not an ounce of litter, no errant barware lost with the throngs, no drunk soldiers left behind. The city has successfully deleted the night before, scrubbed it clean with unseen hands. The breeze carries no aroma of red wine or rain-soaked ska bands. It's almost as if the fiesta never occurred, but we catch a glimpse of the blue and white neckerchief of one clan or another tied to a column of the gazebo. It wasn't all a dream.

We pay our small tab and walk on toward the end of town. A town that's not that big but enough to wake sore bones. As we round the corner out of the municipal plaza, those same green hills that called us to the countryside appear just beyond the end of the road. A corral sits on the right, this is where the running of the bulls begins, *el encierro*. The fences hold no bulls today, the streets, no runners. But there looks to be one last parade. A troupe of musicians and dancers collects just outside the corral, its members clad in the whites and red of Basque tradition.

Flutes and drums tune up as spectators begin to line the roads and balconies along the main street through town. The desolate morning we had first walked into suddenly blossoms into a different type of festive crowd. The music and marching begin in earnest, the dancers gesture and move in unison with wooden swords. We're drawn into the procession marking the true closing ceremony of the *Txikito*.

Just as the parade reaches City Hall, another parade is on a slow-motion collision course with our own. Towering papier-mâché giants and big-headed protectors, the *kilikis* and *zaldikos*. The giants spin and bob along the route, their long skirts whirling over the crowd. Children giggle and run as *kilikis* with soft foam truncheons bop them if they get too close. We run and laugh with the kids and also take a few hits and learn our lesson. This is Pamplona without the need for bulls and a triage nurse, a kinder tradition that precedes Hemingway by a century, one he'd see as pure joy.

The now-merged parades funnel up the hill toward the cathedral. We stick it out until what seems like the religious end and then slip away. San Sebastián calls to us as it did Hemingway to put a bookend on his own fiesta. To rest, to breathe, to eat near his beloved sea. Maybe a swim if these clouds give us a break.

The highway drive to San Sebastián is short, but we opt for Hemingway's more scenic route through the bucolic town of Pasajes. We take a moment to set off on foot through this hamlet and stroll the alleyways, tracing the natural harbor's edge. We happen past the dock where Lafayette sailed to fight in the American Revolutionary War, a house where Victor Hugo once wrote, and a museum where they're rebuilding one of Magellan's boats from a fragment somebody found. Go figure, little old Pasajes is a treasure trove of history without adornment or fanfare.

We walk beyond the end of the town into the wilderness along the water and head toward the open sea. Just to say we did. The trees and the rocks here are ancient, gnarled, worn by the wind and the waves over time. We're a bit winded ourselves and a strong dark coffee back at the town square sets us right as we get back in the car for the quick jump to San Sebastián.

Donostia, as the Basque call the city, is full of life by the time we arrive in early afternoon, and it is pleasant as always. Hemingway wrote, "even on a hot day San Sebastián has a certain early-morning quality. The trees seem as though their leaves were never quite dry." And it is true. The streets glisten as if freshly washed, the air comfortable and crisp in the alleyways of the old town, seldom in the direct sun. Hungry from the seaside hike, we take a seat at a starred restaurant, not by trying, this town is full of them.

The place smells of oakwood smoke and anticipation. Our bottle of Rioja arrives along with a small board of local *idiazabal* cheese and Navarrese sausages. The wine is rich and bright and plays well with the tangy cheese and the meats deep with garlic and spice. The wine brings to mind *Patatas a la Riojana* (page 165). We order some. The stew comes to us in two small crocks, enough to salute Hemingway's preferred wine region, but not so much to overwhelm. Creamy spuds swimming with chorizo in a ruby-red broth is the bite this wine has been waiting for.

The *Salmón con Salsa Béarnaise* (page 163) arrives next, a perfect roast enrobed in sauce béarnaise, skin side still crisp and the flesh like butter. The dish speaks louder in French, but hell, we're close enough and Hemingway loved to reminisce. He once called this fish with this sauce the best he'd ever tasted when he dined at the long-shuttered Restaurante Azaldegui, which was right up the road. *Bon appétit*, as they say a few miles away.

Full and warmed a bit by the wine, we look for the suno and the beach to finish the job. We walk through the rest of the old quarter and onto the promenade above Hemingway's beloved La Concha beach. With a towel and swimsuit in tow we open his playbook, rent a locker, and change.

La Concha is usually a smooth bay protected by the green hill of Santa Clara Island. Today, it's rougher, the waves higher. As Jake Barnes reported before us, "They came in like undulations in the water, gathered weight of water, and then broke smoothly on the warm sand," and warm it was. The water however is bracing on first touch, just a toe, but we then dive in whole. Not quite a polar bear feat, but shocking nevertheless.

We wade out then float farther into the surf, our progress dented a little with each passing roller. Once fully committed, the cold is comfortable, and the blue sky helps. Kids leap and slide from the floating docks, their sounds of delight travel across the surface. Yachts sail in, fishing boats sail out, and we get a few jumps off the docks ourselves.

The sun now focused on our swim, the sea warms around us and so we linger, dive longer and deeper, letting the current sway us to the opposite end of the bay. As we walk the long beach on toasty sand toward the lockers, the sun dries us and leaves us salty. A quick shower, change, then a refreshing shaved ice for the road. As Hemingway's San Sebastián fades in the rearview, a different Pamplona awaits. One where the fiesta is now a memory, but the food is like a siren song. We should not be hungry, and yet here we are.

"The girl came in with the coffee and buttered toast. Or, rather, it was bread toasted and buttered . . . The coffee was good and we drank it out of big bowls. The girl brought in a glass dish of raspberry jam."

—*The Sun Also Rises*

TOSTA CON MANTEQUILLA Y MERMELADA

Raspberry Jam on Toast

TOTAL TIME: 35 minutes
SERVES: 6 to 8 as a side dish

The term marmalade came from the Portuguese *mermelo* for quince, the original sugar-preserved fruit. The process and the word were adopted in Spain and mainly applied to oranges from Sevilla, and today cover all manner of jellies and jams. Here, raspberries, which have only been commercially grown in Spain since 1989, take center stage. Before then, they were cultivated in the wild or imported from France.

RASPBERRY JAM

12 ounces fresh raspberries

⅓ cup honey

1 dash salt

1 tablespoon freshly squeezed lemon juice

6 to 8 slices whole-grain bread, toasted

Salted butter

1 cinnamon stick

Stir all the ingredients except the cinnamon stick into a pot over medium heat. When steam begins to rise from the pot, use a potato masher or fork to mash the berries, leaving some chunks. Reduce the heat to low, add the cinnamon stick, and occasionally stir the mixture as the fruit continues to break down. Simmer and stir for 30 minutes, until the mixture begins to thicken into a syruplike consistency.

Serve the jam warm over hot buttered toast.

"I figured the butter would be good for him."

—*A Moveable Feast*

SALMÓN CON SALSA BÉARNAISE

Broiled Salmon with Béarnaise Sauce

TOTAL TIME: 40 minutes
SERVES: 4 as an entrée

Spain is a major consumer of salmon, but most of the fish comes from Norway and Scotland. Salmon run in the mountainous regions of northern Spain, but not in the quantities that match the demand in Spanish kitchens. Accordingly, most dishes that involve the fish are a nod to international cuisines rather than Spanish traditions.

SALMON

Four 6-ounce salmon fillets

1 tablespoon kosher salt

1 tablespoon extra-virgin olive oil

½ teaspoon freshly ground black pepper

BÉARNAISE SAUCE

¼ cup dry white wine

¼ cup white wine vinegar

1 small shallot, coarsely chopped

2 to 3 sprigs fresh tarragon, leaves and stems divided, leaves minced

3 large egg yolks

¼ teaspoon kosher salt

¼ teaspoon freshly ground black pepper

8 tablespoons unsalted butter, melted

Crusty bread, for serving

TO START THE SALMON: Dust the salmon fillets with 1 tablespoon of salt and set aside for 30 minutes on a paper-towel-lined plate.

TO MAKE THE BÉARNAISE SAUCE: Add the wine, vinegar, shallot, and tarragon stems to a small pot over medium-high heat. Bring the mixture to a boil, then reduce the heat to low. Simmer for 15 minutes, stirring occasionally.

Pour the mixture through a fine-mesh strainer into the bowl of a blender, pressing down on the solids to extract as much liquid as possible. Add the egg yolks, salt, and pepper to the blender and blend at medium speed. Open the top portal of the blender and, while running, slowly pour in the butter. Once all the butter is incorporated, close the top and turn the blender to high for 1 minute. Transfer the béarnaise sauce to a small pot over low heat, stir in the minced tarragon, and cover.

TO FINISH THE SALMON: Set the broiler to high and place a rack 6 inches below the element. Rinse the fillets in cold water and pat dry with paper towels. Brush the fillets with olive oil and season with black pepper. Brush a baking sheet with olive oil and place the fillets skin-side up on the pan. Brush oil across the skin. Broil for 4 to 5 minutes, until the skin is darkened, slightly bubbled, but not burnt. Carefully remove the fillets from under the broiler and flip them skin-side down.

Return the fillets to under the broiler and continue to cook for 1 to 2 minutes, until the flesh side is light pink. Remove from under the broiler and plate, skin-side up. Let the salmon rest for 5 minutes. Pour the béarnaise sauce over the fillets and serve warm with crusty bread to soak up any extra sauce.

"Rioja is wine of the Rioja region in the north of Spain; both red and white wines. The best are those of the Bodegas Bilbaínos, Marqués de Murrieta, Marqués de Riscal. Rioja Clarete, or Rioja Alta are the lightest and pleasantest of the red wines."

—*Death in the Afternoon*

PATATAS A LA RIOJANA
Rioja Potato Stew

TOTAL TIME: 1 hour
SERVES: 6 to 8 as a tapa or an appetizer, 3 to 5 as a side dish

La Rioja is known for its nation-defining wines throughout the world, and the region's cuisine typically uses local wine as an identifying ingredient. *Patatas a la Riojana* does not. It is simply a dish originally crafted by laborers to stave off the cold during relatively harsh winter months while prepping the vineyards for spring. But the name itself carries the air of quality and spread throughout Spain.

¼ cup extra-virgin olive oil

1 large onion, diced

1 large green bell pepper, diced

3 cloves garlic, minced

2 links Spanish chorizo or other smoked sausage, cut into ½-inch disks

1½ pounds Yukon Gold potatoes, cut into 2-inch chunks

1 tablespoon smoked paprika

2 teaspoons kosher salt

4 cups chicken stock

2 tablespoons minced parsley, for garnish

Crusty bread, for serving

Add the olive oil to a Dutch oven or large pot over medium-high heat. When the oil begins to shimmer, add the onion and sauté until translucent, about 8 to 10 minutes. Add the bell pepper, garlic, and sausage and continue to sauté for 5 minutes. Add the potatoes, paprika, and salt and sauté for an additional 3 minutes. Add the stock or water, increase the heat to high, and bring to a boil. Reduce the heat to medium-low and maintain a strong simmer for 20 to 25 minutes, until the potatoes are easily pierced with a knife.

Serve the stew hot on a cold day, garnished with parsley, alongside crusty bread.

CHAPTER 20

THE BULL

Hemingway's Encierro

"There were so many people running ahead of the bulls that the mass thickened and slowed up going through the gate into the ring, and as the bulls passed, galloping together, heavy, muddy-sided, horns swinging, one shot ahead, caught a man in the running crowd in the back and lifted him in the air. Both the man's arms were by his sides, his head went back as the horn went in, and the bull lifted him and then dropped him."

—*The Sun Also Rises*

We ascend into Pamplona once again, the setting sun seems to follow the car. The grand facade of the Plaza de Toros rises above the street, its white walls catching the fading light like a bull taking its final bow.

We pull through the square straight up to the La Perla lobby and the valet makes the car disappear. The air has cooled and sharpened as we begin another attempt at our *encierro* walk. This is the route the bulls run to the ring each morning during the big San Fermín, the same path where countless humans believe they can outrun, outsmart, and outlast the stampede. We had started our comparatively lazy version this morning near the corral but were whisked into an unexpected parade, the best kind of interruption.

Strolling the path in reverse this time seems right, starting at the bullring and toward the corral. It would have been a great choice for many bulls, too, we think as we stare into Hemingway's stony-eyed statue outside the arena gates. Following his gaze, we cross the way and enter Estafeta Street, the longest section of the run. It's straight and wide with no hindrances, hills, or places to hide. We take a moment at the top of the stretch to look at the stone tiles that line the street, pockmarked, dented, scratched by thousands of thundering hooves over time.

We chase one another down the street, two index fingers as horns, melodramatically shrieking and dodging a mock goring. An older gentleman laughs with us as we roar past his front-stoop stool, his personal wine bar for the evening. "You're going the wrong way," he shouts after us. We pause and disarm our fingers. "Have you run with the bulls?" we ask. "That's a young man's game and I'm too old," he quips, "and too smart." And, so, we run on, index fingers back on charge.

At the end of Estafeta lies the riskiest section of the run, "Dead Man's Curve," that treacherous turn on the path where bulls and runners alike crash against the stone, at times on top of one another. It feels heavy here, as though the air itself holds the memory of all the bruises and breaks earned in this space. We notice Iruñazarra just across the square. The restaurant's name means "Old Pamplona" and feels ironic for a place so new, yet it holds the weight of tradition, and the scuttlebutt says the best steaks in town. In a decidedly macabre moment, we head in to reenact Hemingway's last meal.

Hemingway wasn't immune to the occasional comedy of death. The man reveled in reading his own obituary after *surviving* two plane crashes in Africa within two days, the world temporarily unaware. News did not travel fast in those days. Back to the last meal.

The now infamous dinner was enjoyed with his wife Mary at Christiania's in Ketchum, Idaho. A New York strip

steak grilled rare, no sauce, Caesar salad, baked potato, and Bordeaux. Simple and easy to replicate, though with a Basque accent this time. Inside, the bar hums with life, the kind of buzz that comes from good friends and good food. We imagine Hemingway here, adding to the clamor, waiting on excellent meat, with a glass of red in hand watching a sea of revelers pass through the square. His happy place, indeed.

On offer is not Hemingway's grilled strip steak, *Lomo Alto a la Parrilla* (page 168), but they say the *chuletón* here is legendary. A great big thick cut pretty close to a T-bone, yet far enough away to be unique. We also order a green salad and roasted *Patatas Bravas* (page 171) on the side like miniature baked potatoes, and, of course, a bottle of Bordeaux. Being a stone's throw from France makes that okay. The dishes arrive all at once, with all the warmth, aroma, and sizzle that portend a great meal.

Everything is executed perfectly, our hats off to the chef. The steak, tender and unadorned but for sweet peppers. They count as a vegetable, though the salad is just fine too. The *chuletón* tastes of beef and not sauce, the way he liked it. Its edges charred but its heart still red, a testament to the animal's sacrifice. The potatoes are crisp, the sauce savory and as spicy as Spain will allow. Not very spicy, which makes the "*bravas*" title brave itself. Perhaps better to say *patatas bravas* honor the courage of the bull-runners.

The Bordeaux is the right complement, deep and dark, heady and complex. A glass invites reflection. As we eat and sip, we continue to see Hemingway here, taking joy in the atmosphere, his eyes alight not with despair but with the deep satisfaction of a man savoring life's simple pleasures.

We emerge from the restaurant into the square, the spires of the cathedral catch the moonlight. The bells toll, a solemn rhythm that seems both an ending and a beginning. The festival has passed, and the bars and terraces are again alive, now with everyday cheer; cigarettes glow like fireflies, and glasses clink as though Spain itself is toasting this night.

Hemingway once wrote that Spain was the country he loved most after his own, and as we walk here, his reasons are clear. This is a place that embraces life fully, its passions, its risks, its fleeting beauty. Maybe a night like this would have helped stave off Hemingway's battles just a little longer and offered another story to tell. Maybe not.

As we wind our way down Santo Domingo Street and reach the corral, the start of the *encierro*, there is no gathering parade, not a person, no noise. Only a moment of peace.

> *"The world is a fine place and worth the fighting for and I hate very much to leave it."*
>
> —*For Whom the Bell Tolls*

"You can eat at booths where they grill steaks and roast chickens over a charcoal fire and drink all the Valdapeñas wine you can hold."

—*Death in the Afternoon*

LOMO ALTO A LA PARRILLA

Grilled New York Strip Steak

TOTAL TIME: 2 hours, 10 minutes

SERVES: 6 to 8 as a tapa, 2 to 3 as an entrée

Bovine have been raised throughout Spain for centuries, mainly for field work and bullfighting. But in northern Spain, Galicia and Basque Country are famous for beef cattle that never met a plow or the bullring. Famous steaks include the *Rubia Gallega* and the *Txuleton*, both rib cuts, usually very thick and cooked over a live fire. Here, we take a relatively small cut and treat it in a very Spanish fashion.

STEAK

1 tablespoon smoked paprika

1 teaspoon dried rosemary

½ teaspoon garlic powder

½ teaspoon onion powder

1½ teaspoons kosher salt

Two 10-ounce New York strip steaks, 1 inch thick

PEPPERS

2 cloves garlic, peeled

½ cup extra-virgin olive oil

8 jarred *piquillo* peppers, julienned, or 2 red bell peppers, roasted, peeled, seeded, and julienned

TO PREPARE THE STEAK: In a food processor, pulverize the paprika, rosemary, garlic powder, onion powder, and salt. Coat the steaks with the mixture and set them on a rack over a baking sheet for 2 hours.

TO MAKE THE PEPPERS: Preheat the oven to 350°F. Put the garlic cloves and olive oil in a small, rimmed baking dish or oven-safe skillet. Transfer into the oven and roast for 15 to 20 minutes, until the garlic looks toasted. Remove from the oven and use a slotted spoon to remove the garlic cloves from the dish. Reduce the oven temperature to 250°F.

Add the peppers into the baking dish in a single layer and ensure they are coated with oil. Transfer the vessel back into the oven and roast for 1 hour.

Remove the baking dish from the oven and reset to broil. Set the oven rack about 6 inches from the heating element. Carefully transfer the baking dish or skillet to the oven and broil the peppers until they are barely charred, about 2 to 3 minutes. Remove from the oven and set aside.

TO FINISH THE STEAKS: Prepare the grill to high heat and oil the grill grates. Set the steaks on the grill and cook for 4 minutes—2 minutes before rotating the steaks 45 degrees to obtain a crosshatch pattern on the crust, then another 2 minutes. Flip the steaks and cook for 4 minutes more. Use tongs to sear the edges of the steaks, especially the fat-cap, for 1 minute, until browned.

Remove the steaks from the grill and let them sit for at least 10 minutes. Slice the steaks at ¼ inch across the grain and plate along with the cooked peppers.

"There is no sure sign by which bravery may be determined although there are many indications of probable cowardice."

—*Death in the Afternoon*

PATATAS BRAVAS
Roasted Potatoes with "Brave" Sauce

TOTAL TIME: 50 minutes
SERVES: 4 to 6 as a tapa or an appetizer, 2 to 3 as a side dish

Patatas bravas are typically some format of crisp potato chunks served with a red sauce and a white sauce for dipping or swiping. It is frequently noted on menus that the red sauce is spicy, as *"bravas"* can mean ferocious, angry, or brave. Piquant, perhaps, but to the American palate, the sauce is neither ferocious nor angry, and definitely not spicy.

POTATOES

8 ounces fingerling potatoes, topped and tailed

2 tablespoons extra-virgin olive oil

½ teaspoon kosher salt

SALSA BRAVA
(MAKES ABOUT 1 CUP)

¾ cup ketchup

3 jarred *piquillo* peppers or 1 roasted red bell pepper, peeled and seeded

2 cloves garlic or ½ teaspoon garlic powder

½ teaspoon onion powder

1 teaspoon smoked paprika

½ teaspoon kosher salt

½ teaspoon red chile flakes (optional)

1 tablespoon extra-virgin olive oil

ALIOLI CLÁSICO
(MAKES ABOUT 1 CUP)

1 large egg

1 tablespoon sherry, white wine, or rice vinegar

2 cloves garlic or ½ teaspoon garlic powder

½ teaspoon kosher salt

¾ cup vegetable oil

TO MAKE THE POTATOES: Preheat the oven to 425°F. In a large mixing bowl, toss the potatoes with the olive oil and salt. Stand each fingerling potato on its end on a baking sheet. Transfer to the oven and roast for 35 to 45 minutes, until the potatoes are cooked through and crispy. Remove the potatoes from the oven.

TO MAKE THE *ALIOLI CLÁSICO*: If using an immersion blender, place all the ingredients in a clear round container that just fits the blades of an immersion blender (such as a liquid measuring cup). Hold the blades of the blender flat against the bottom of the container and turn it on. As you observe white gel forming at the bottom of the container, slowly raise the blades straight up following the growth of the white gel. Once you reach the surface of the alioli, all the ingredients should be combined. Blend in drops of water as needed to create a condiment texture.

If using a countertop blender, add the egg, sherry, garlic, and salt to the blender and turn to medium speed. Open the top portal of the blender and, while running, slowly pour in the oil. Once all the oil is incorporated, close the top and turn the blender to high speed for 1 minute. Blend in drops of water as needed to create a condiment texture.

TO MAKE THE *SALSA BRAVA*: Using a countertop blender or immersion blender, purée all the ingredients.

Serve the potatoes hot, topped with *salsa brava* and *alioli clásico*.

CHAPTER 21

THE FIRST MEAL IN SPAIN

"The first meal in Spain was always a shock with the hors d'oeuvres, an egg course, two meat courses, vegetables, salad, and dessert and fruit. You have to drink plenty of wine to get it all down."

—The Sun Also Rises

Ernest Hemingway loved Spanish food. Not just for its offered satisfaction, though delicious is delicious, but for what it represented. Food in Spain is more than sustenance. It's a celebration of life. It's about love, community, camaraderie, true friendships, and the occasional party. Or perhaps the every-night party. Cooking here lies at the intersection of land and sea, shaped by those whose hands work both. It's how Hemingway celebrated a good bullfight and how he mourned a bad one. It is an art form, albeit simple and straightforward, as evocative as the paintings and literature that define the country and inspired the man. As if food were a religion itself.

Hemingway didn't write much about food in grand detail. Instead, he wrote about the world it inhabits, the joy, the grief, the ritual, where food is another essential character, moving the story forward. In *The Sun Also Rises*, Hemingway offers a brief but telling primer on Spanish food. As Jake Barnes and his companions-in-dysfunction arrive in Pamplona, he lists the courses of their first meal: hors d'oeuvres, eggs, meat, vegetables, salad, dessert, and fruit. It's more than a passing mention. It's an invitation to his Spanish table, an introduction to Spain's culinary soul.

For what it's worth, Pamplona was the first town named for Pompey the Great, so things could have gone much worse for Barnes's crew than Robert Cohn. We digress.

We find it poetic to experience this "first meal" as our last of the journey. We began in Madrid at Sobrino de Botín with the final meal from the same book, and we've taken his path in reverse. Now, we look out at the Plaza de Toros, where Hemingway began his affair with this country. The restaurant is El Burladero, aptly named for the wooden barrier that offers matadors refuge in the bullring. It's the perfect place to reflect and feast.

Hemingway did us a favor by keeping his description of the meal vague, a simple list of courses allows for a bit of flexibility. At El Burladero, the terrace is elegant, the energy congenial, and the menu spectacular. We craft a lingering meal worthy of our own grand finale. For wine, we return to Rioja Alta, Hemingway's vino of tempranillo, the "noble grape," and a classic choice that pairs seamlessly with the region's cuisine.

For hors d'oeuvres, we begin with the *Pintxo de Gilda* (page 178), a quintessential tapa named for Rita Hayworth's sultry character in the 1946 film of the same name. A single skewer, it layers an olive, a pickled pepper, and an anchovy. A perfect bite of salty, piquant pleasure. We order it because it's a favorite, but also as a nod to Hemingway's "frenemy," Orson Welles, Hayworth's greatest love. Alongside, we order a simple charcuterie board of cured meats and cheeses, showcasing Spain's mastery of preservation and flavor.

Eggs come next. The dish is *Revueltos de Hongos* (page 179), Spanish-style scrambled eggs cooked with wild mushrooms until creamy and rich. Almost as much vegetable as egg, a unique formula in a world of scrambles. The choice is a

challenge, as Spain also has an under-sung mastery of eggs, and the options are vast. The next dish offers to come with a fried egg on top, but we choose not to, don't want to overly egg. It's *Pisto* (page 174), Spain's answer to ratatouille, a medley of eggplant, tomatoes, peppers, and onions, we keep it in the vegetable column, and on a slab of bread.

For meat, we go for two dishes that speak to the depth of Spanish cooking. The first is *Carrilleras con Pimientos Cristal* (page 177), stewed pork cheeks that melt in the mouth, served with sweet roasted peppers and crunchy potato straws. A bit reminiscent of a Cuban *mojo* pork, Hemingway would have been pleased. As a salute to Hemingway the hunter, the second meat is *Perdiz Escabechada* (page 180), partridge cooked and preserved in a tangy broth of vinegar, oil, and herbs. The dish arrives cold, accompanied by a crisp, simple salad that balances the richness of the other courses. It's brighter than we expect—the Spanish love vinegar.

Dessert brings us to a Basque classic, *Tarta de Queso* (page 183), the "burnt" cheesecake, with its caramelized crust and creamy interior. The beauty of the Basque masterpiece is the distinct lack of an actual crust; it's just the outside taking all the heat and keeping the inside safe. It's served with fresh fruit on the side, though we're purists at heart and enjoy the cheesecake on its own. A round of *café con leche* follows, the perfect conclusion to a meal that satisfies in the memory as much as it does on the palate.

First, middle, or last, this meal was going to be a shock any time it was had. We roll off the terrace and across the street to visit Ernest one last time before we depart. His statue sits as if protecting the bullring, with his stare fixed at Castillo Square and the old town beyond. As we sit perched on the edges of the pedestal holding up his stone bust and steely glance, we reflect on the journey, on Hemingway, on basking in the magnificence of Madrid, the bittersweetness of Sevilla, the romance of Ronda, the down-to-earth feeling of Valencia, and ending in Pamplona, a city of enduring magic.

There's a rightness to ending here.

"He felt much healthier in the war, probably due to the forced curtailment of the number of meat courses."

—*For Whom the Bell Tolls*

PISTO
Ratatouille

TOTAL TIME: 45 minutes
SERVES: 10 to 12 as a tapa, 4 to 6 as a side dish

The word *pisto* is from the same base as *pesto* and *pestle*. They all mean to mash or pound. In Spain, this means to take all the spring and summer vegetables and cook them in their own juices until they're closer to a paste than their original form. French *ratatouille* comes from the word to stir. Generally, the same vegetables, but less destruction.

9 tablespoons extra-virgin olive oil, divided

1 eggplant, diced

1 teaspoon kosher salt, divided

1 onion, diced

3 jarred *piquillo* peppers, diced or 1 red bell pepper, roasted, peeled, seeded, and diced

2 tablespoons tomato paste

1 medium tomato, diced

½ teaspoon freshly ground black pepper

Preheat the oven to 375°F.

Add 4 tablespoons of olive oil to a Dutch oven or other oven-safe pot over medium heat. When the oil begins to shimmer, add the eggplant and ½ teaspoon of salt and sauté until the eggplant is soft and begins to brown, about 4 to 6 minutes. Remove the cooked eggplant from the pot.

Add 2 tablespoons of olive oil. When the oil begins to shimmer, add the onion and sauté until it is translucent, about 6 to 8 minutes. Stir in the roasted peppers and tomato paste and continue to sauté for 2 minutes. Remove the pot from the heat and stir in the cooked eggplant, tomato, black pepper, the remaining 3 tablespoons of olive oil, and the remaining ½ teaspoon of salt.

Transfer the pot to the oven and roast until the vegetables on top are just beginning to gain color, about 20 to 25 minutes.

Remove the *pisto* from the oven and serve hot or at room temperature as an accompaniment to meat, fish, or atop crusty bread.

GRAN OFERTA

Narrator:	*"I have some meat for all of us, and we can cook it in the room."*
John:	*"I cook it, I cook good. I remember one time when I cook on ship . . ."*
Narrator:	*"It will be pretty tough. It's just been freshly butchered."*
John:	*"Is a no such thing as a tough meat in a war."*

—"THE DENUNCIATION," *THE FIFTH COLUMN*

CARRILLERAS CON PIMIENTOS CRISTAL

Braised Pork Cheeks and Peppers

TOTAL TIME: 4 hours
SERVES: 4 to 6 as an entrée

If you recall, the *bOOmVeja* shredded-lamb dish that comes in a smoky bomb to the bar is a showstopper at Baserriberri in Pamplona. That's the *pintxo* of notoriety, but their *carrilleras*, stewed pork cheeks, is the standout entrée in the formal dining room. We enjoyed it viscerally and yielded yet another recipe conversation with our friend and Baserriberri manager, Javier Sánchez, who says Chef Iñaki Andradas's creative side comes out to play here as well. As is a modern restaurant tactic, Chef Iñaki cooks large quantities of meat *sous vide* over several hours to achieve the perfect temperature before a final braise. We offer a more home-friendly version below, yet we keep his immaculate sauce intact.

24 to 28 ounces pork cheeks, trimmed of fatty membranes and cut into 4 portions

2 teaspoons kosher salt, divided

1 teaspoon freshly ground black pepper, divided

2 tablespoons extra-virgin olive oil

1 large white onion, julienned

1 large carrot, julienned

2 cloves garlic, minced

1 large tomato, diced

2 cups dry red wine

1 cup beef stock

2 teaspoons cornstarch

1 recipe of *Pimientos del Piquillo Confitados* (page 111), julienned for service

8 ounces potato straws, for service

Minced chives, for garnish

Preheat the oven to 320°F. Evenly season the cheeks with 1 teaspoon of salt and ½ teaspoon of pepper. Add olive oil to a Dutch oven over medium-high heat. When the oil begins to shimmer, brown the cheeks, about 2 to 3 minutes per side. Remove the cheeks to a plate.

Add the onion and carrot to the pot and sauté for 6 to 8 minutes, until well browned. Add the garlic and tomato and continue to sauté for 4 to 5 minutes. Pour in the wine, bring to a boil for 8 to 10 minutes, until reduced by about one-quarter. Add stock and the remaining salt and pepper, and return to a boil. Add the seared cheeks to the pot, cover, and transfer to the oven for 3 to 3½ hours, until the pork pulls away easily with a fork. Remove the pot from the oven and use a slotted spoon to remove just the cheeks to a plate.

Transfer the remaining contents of the pot to a blender and purée. Strain the sauce and return to the pot over high heat. In a small glass, mix cornstarch with ¼ cup of water. When the sauce reaches a boil, stir in the cornstarch mixture by the tablespoon until a desired sauce consistency is reached. Turn off the heat. Return the cheeks to the pot and cover to keep warm.

To serve, plate a portion of cheek with some sauce, a scoop of roasted peppers, and some potato straws. Garnish with chives.

"The waiter brought them glasses of manzanilla from the lowland near Cadiz called the Marismas with thin slices of jamón serrano, a smoky, hard cured ham from pigs that fed on acorns . . . and anchovies and garlic olives. They ate these and drank more of the manzanilla, which was light and nutty tasting."

—*The Garden of Eden*

PINTXO DE GILDA

Skewer of Olive, Pepper, and Anchovy

TOTAL TIME: 5 minutes
SERVES: 2 as a tapa or an appetizer

This simple dish of olive, pepper, and anchovy is said to have been the original *pintxo*, or skewered snack, from Basque Country. A crafty restaurateur devised a perfect bite that was equally strong, salty, and spicy, just like Rita Hayworth's character in the movie *Gilda*. It is also just acidic enough to open the palate for any dish that follows.

4 green Manzanilla or other olives, pitted

4 pickled *guindilla* or banana peppers (sliced into strips), stemmed

2 anchovy fillets

Extra-virgin olive oil, for drizzling

On 2 short skewers, like those piercing an olive in a martini, creatively stack olives, peppers, and anchovies. The perfect Gilda is a single bite, so placing the anchovy and even the peppers in an "S" pattern on the skewer helps. Drizzle the skewers with plenty of olive oil and serve.

"We got an imperial quart of good Gibraltar whiskey from the car and all had whiskey and mineral water against the cold, wet night. We had two drinks apiece while they found us some fair tenderloin and cooked some eggs and brought a soup."

—*The Dangerous Summer*

REVUELTOS DE HONGOS
Scrambled Eggs with Mushrooms

TOTAL TIME: 20 minutes
SERVES: 3 to 4 as a tapa or an appetizer, 2 as an entrée

In Spain, the egg is queen and is never alone. She intermingles with potatoes, cured meats, and/or vegetables in various formats. This could be a *tortilla*, cousin to the frittata; *estrellados*, a "starry" fried egg with beaming whites; *rotos*—a "broken" fried egg mixed in with the other players; or *revueltos*, eggs scrambled with a supporting cast. The queen is also not a morning person.

- 5 large eggs
- 1½ tablespoons whole milk
- ½ teaspoon kosher salt, divided
- 2 tablespoons extra-virgin olive oil
- ½ small onion, diced
- 12 ounces assorted wild mushrooms, washed and thinly sliced
- 2 cloves garlic, minced
- 1 tablespoon minced parsley
- Baguette slices, for serving

In a mixing bowl, whisk together the eggs, milk, and ¼ teaspoon of salt and set aside. Leave a bit of egg white unincorporated for a more dramatic-looking final dish.

Add the olive oil to a skillet over medium-high heat. When the oil begins to shimmer, add the onion and sauté for 3 to 4 minutes, until it just begins to brown at the edges. Add the mushrooms, garlic, and the remaining ½ teaspoon of salt and continue to sauté for an additional 6 to 8 minutes, until the mushrooms are cooked through. Reduce the heat to medium-low, pour in the egg mixture and scramble together, stirring occasionally, for 5 to 8 minutes, until the egg is just set.

Transfer the creamy scramble to a serving plate, garnish with parsley, and serve warm with bread slices for stacking.

"Shiny and spotted, they were plump and fresh and firm-fleshed and you could pick out your own trout and partridges in the kitchen."

—*The Dangerous Summer*

ENSALADA DE PERDIZ ESCABECHADA

Poached Partridge with Salad

TOTAL TIME: 2 hours
SERVES: 4 as an entrée

The king of Sevilla hotel fame, Alfonso XIII, formalized partridge hunting in Spain in the late 1800s. Today, toward the start of the shooting season in mid fall, one spies the bird in many forms on restaurant menus. Given the partridge's leanness, it lends itself to poaching in an acidic mixture, thereby retaining moisture. This is a blink-and-you'll-miss-it dish.

ESCABECHADA

Two 10-to-12-ounce partridges, split in 2, or 1 Cornish game hen, split into 2 breasts, 2 legs

2 teaspoons kosher salt

½ cup extra-virgin olive oil, divided

1 large onion, diced

1 carrot, diced

6 cloves garlic

2 teaspoons dried rosemary

2 teaspoons dried thyme

12 black peppercorns

1 cup white wine

1 cup apple cider vinegar

SALAD

8 ounces mixed salad greens

11 ounces cherry tomatoes, halved

1 cup cooked corn kernels

2 tablespoons extra-virgin olive oil

¼ cup apple cider vinegar

¼ teaspoon kosher salt

TO MAKE THE *ESCABECHADA*: Evenly season the bird portions with 1 teaspoon of salt. Add ¼ cup of olive oil to a pot over medium-high heat. When the oil begins to shimmer, sear the bird portions, about 1 to 2 minutes per side, until lightly browned. Do not overcrowd the pot and repeat if necessary. Remove the bird portions with a slotted spoon to a plate.

Add the remaining ¼ cup of olive oil to the pot. When it begins to shimmer, add the onion, carrot, garlic, rosemary, thyme, and peppercorns to the pot, reduce the heat to medium, and sauté for 8 to 10 minutes, until they begin to caramelize.

Place the seared-bird portions back in the pot, followed by the wine, 1 cup of water, and the vinegar, along with the remaining 1 teaspoon of salt. Increase the heat to high and bring to a boil. Reduce the heat to low, cover the pot, and let simmer for 75 to 90 minutes, until the bird portions are cooked through and a fork easily peels away the meat. Remove just the bird portions from the pot to a plate and, when cool, pat dry with paper towels.

Transfer the remaining contents of the pot to a blender and purée. Allow both the meat and the sauce to cool separately, as the flavors improve the cooler they are.

TO MAKE THE SALAD: Place the mixed greens, tomatoes, and corn in a large bowl and combine. Just before serving, drizzle with the olive oil and vinegar, add the salt, and toss lightly. Serve a portion of *escabechada* draped in the blended sauce, along with some salad.

"Nay. Thou art lovely. Thou hast a lovely face and a beautiful body, long and light, and thy skin is smooth and the color of burnt gold and every one will try to take thee from me."

—*For Whom the Bell Tolls*

TARTA DE QUESO
Basque "Burnt" Cheesecake

TOTAL TIME: 2 hours, 25 minutes
SERVES: 8 to 10 as a dessert

The Basque cheesecake was first brought to popularity by La Viña restaurant in San Sebastián in the nineties, and the internet made it viral. With its sweet, creamy interior and crisp, slightly bitter outer shell, it was unique in a world of cheesecakes with separate crusts. This custard makes its own crust by ever-so-slightly burning, keeping the delicate center encased. If you go back far enough, the Romans had a similar idea, but no social media.

- 2 pounds cream cheese, at room temperature
- 1¼ cups sugar
- 7 large eggs
- 2 cups heavy cream
- ½ cup all-purpose flour
- 1 teaspoon kosher salt
- 1 tablespoon vegetable oil

Preheat the oven to 400°F.

In the bowl of a stand mixer fitted with a paddle, cream the cream cheese and sugar on medium speed until the sugar has fully dissolved, about 4 to 5 minutes. Add the eggs one at a time until they are all blended in. Scrape down the sides of the bowl as needed to ensure an even, consistent mixture. Pour in the cream at low speed and allow it to incorporate fully. Sprinkle the flour and salt across the top and continue to mix until the batter is extremely smooth, about 5 minutes.

Grease the insides of a Dutch oven with oil, then line with parchment paper. It is wise to use 2 sheets of parchment in opposite directions to ensure that the batter will be fully encased as it bakes and rises. Pour the batter into the paper-lined pot and transfer it to the oven. Bake until the top is deep, dark brown, about 60 to 70 minutes.

Remove the cake from the oven and let it rest at room temperature for 1 hour. Carefully lift it out of the pot using the parchment paper as handles. Gently pull the parchment away from the sides of the cake. Slice warm, jiggly slices of cheesecake and serve.

EPILOGUE
BARCELONA

"Catalonia is Spain, but the people are not Spanish and although bullfighting flourishes in Barcelona it is on a fake basis because the public that attends goes as to a circus for excitement and entertainment and is as ignorant, almost, as the publics of Nîmes, Béziers and Arles. The Catalans have a rich country, a great part of it at least; they are good farmers, good businessmen, good salesmen; they are the commercially elect of Spain. The richer the country the simpler the peasantry and they combine a simple peasantry and a childish language, with a highly developed commercial class. With them . . . life is too practical for there to be much of the hardest kind of common sense nor much feeling about death."

—*Death in the Afternoon*

We rise as the morning mist barely yields to the autumn sun and with these sure signs of new beginnings, we say goodbye to Pamplona. The air is crisp, pure, and abundant as we drive away from Castillo Square with the windows down just to breathe as much Navarrese clarity as we can before heading to Barcelona. It's different there and Hemingway felt it too.

His relationship with Barcelona was complicated. The city was never quite Spanish to him, but rather Catalan, different in spirit, fractured by politics, and marked by infighting. Reporting from the city during the Spanish Civil War, he saw those divisions firsthand. "You should see Barcelona," he wrote in *For Whom the Bell Tolls*. "It is still comic opera. First, it was the paradise of the crackpots and the romantic revolutionists. Now it is the paradise of the fake soldier. The soldiers who like to wear uniforms, who like to strut and swagger and wear red-and-black scarves. Who like everything about war except to fight."

He believed that the anarchists and Loyalists' infighting weakened their resistance to Franco, leaving Barcelona, and the Republic, vulnerable. He watched the city suffer, devastated by Franco's bombs and the betrayal of its own ideals. Wartime Barcelona, for Hemingway, carried the weight of both political *and* personal strife, as his marriage to Pauline Pfeiffer was unraveling amidst his growing attachment to Martha Gellhorn. Over time, tales of Hemingway's happier times in Barcelona endure, holding court at the Majestic Hotel bar, sunset daiquiris atop the Avenida Palace, absinthe with Picasso and Dalí at Bar Marsella.

Beverage stories duly spoken for, we walk the city in search of Hemingway's Spanish table, but out of focus. Foods he loved but may have challenged his culinary sensibilities, foods that fly in the face of the traditions to which he grew attached. The historic center, an expected Hemingway neighborhood, is our first stop. Bar del Pla, tucked into the Gothic Quarter, bustles with locals and tourists alike. The *Tortilla Vaga de Bacalao* (page 188), a "lazy" *tortilla Española*, is on the menu. Today's version features salt-cod and Navarrese crystal peppers, displayed proudly on top rather than buried beneath the eggs. The flavors are bold and true, though Hemingway might have scoffed at calling it a *tortilla* at all.

We move on to Sarrià, just into the hills, a neighborhood of expats and quiet terraces, a very Hemingway formula. At Keik Cafè , we sit in the sun with cold beers and a dish

Hemingway might guess to recognize but never expect, *Langostino Wonton* (page 186), shrimp wrapped in Asian-style noodles and fried crisp. The plate arrives with a bright sauce of passion fruit and coconut. The shrimp is perfect, its plating playful, but it leans far from the simply grilled or sizzling shrimp that fueled Hemingway while gazing at the sea. Perhaps he'd grumble at the innovation, but after a few crunches and succulent bites, and another beer, he might agree it's worth eating.

Descending into L'Eixample, we find Soma, a small restaurant with a working-class spirit and lacking the pretension Hemingway avoided. It feels like the kind of place he might have lingered in if not for the menu featuring *socarrat*, the golden crust of a perfect *paella*, reimagined as savory cookies, *Galletas de Socarrat* (page 189). Topped with pickled peppers, garlic aioli, and fresh oregano, the dish is clever and delicious, but far afield from the communal essence of *paella*, spooned from the pan under a Valencian sky. Hemingway, ever the romantic, might have bristled at the transformation, but the taste is undeniably good.

We return to the Gothic Quarter and Sant Felip Neri Square, a small plaza scarred by Francoist bombing. The surrounding walls, gouged by shrapnel, stand as a testament to the war's toll. We sit on the terrace facing Hemingway's memory. Here, a modern bistro thankfully changes the vibe with a *Tatín de Rabo de Buey* (page 191). The oxtail, braised and reduced to a pâté-like layer, is fused atop flaky pastry with apples, some roasted, some puréed. The flavors are rich and deep, honoring Andalusian tradition even as the format breaks from it. Hemingway, who revered the bull in life and death, might have appreciated the homage, especially after a glass or two of Valdepeñas. Maybe a third if he's facing this wall.

The day ends, as it must, at Bar Marsella in the Raval neighborhood. The atmosphere is timeless, the cracked mirrors and dusty bottles conjure a sense of history unvarnished. Hemingway nursed the green fairy here, the licorice-scented solace dulling the sharp edges of a city that left him with more questions than answers. "Absinthe made everything seem better," he wrote, and as the sugary drips of water cloud our drinks, we agree and toast to the man who gave us his Spain, unvarnished.

"At noon we were all at the café. It was crowded. We were eating shrimps and drinking beer. The town was crowded. Every street was full."

—*The Sun Also Rises*

LANGOSTINO WONTON

Fried Shrimp in Noodles

TOTAL TIME: 45 minutes
SERVES: 6 to 10 as a tapa or an appetizer

As Hemingway would attest, Spain loves its shrimp. Branching out from the stalwarts of sizzling garlic shrimp, grilled prawns, and those nestled within rice dishes, Spanish cooks began looking outside the borders. Modern tapas menus regularly feature examples like tempura, curry, and carpaccio. This crispy noodle-wrapped version is fairly unique.

SHRIMP

10 large shrimp, peeled and deveined

¼ teaspoon baking soda

½ teaspoon freshly ground black pepper

3 teaspoons kosher salt, divided

1 pound wide, flat egg noodles, such as linguine or fettuccine

Vegetable oil, for frying

PASSION-COCONUT SAUCE

½ cup coconut cream

2 teaspoons cornstarch

1 cup frozen passion fruit purée, thawed

2 teaspoons honey

2 teaspoons sugar

¼ teaspoon kosher salt

1 tablespoon cold, unsalted butter

TO START THE SHRIMP: Season the shrimp with the baking soda, black pepper, and 1 teaspoon of salt, and set aside for 30 minutes. Prepare the noodles.

Cook the noodles according to package instructions with the remaining 2 teaspoons of salt to al dente. Drain and rinse the noodles with cold water to rid them of excess starch. Lay the noodles straightened in a single layer on paper towels to dry.

TO MAKE THE PASSION-COCONUT SAUCE: In a mixing bowl, whisk together the coconut cream and cornstarch and set aside. Add the passion fruit purée, honey, sugar, and salt to a pot over medium heat. When the sugar and salt dissolve, stir in the coconut cream mixture. Increase heat to medium-high and bring the mixture to a boil and stir in the butter until it melts. Remove from the heat and set aside.

TO FINISH THE SHRIMP: Wrap each shrimp completely in cooked and cooled noodles in a single layer and set aside on a plate. Do not stack. Loose ends are okay, but assure the shrimp packages do not unravel before you cook them.

Pour enough oil into a skillet to about 1 inch in depth. Heat the oil to 350°F over medium heat. If you do not have a thermometer, one handy trick is to use a wooden chopstick. As the oil heats, touch the tip of the chopstick to the bottom of the skillet at an angle. Once you see lots of bubbles forming around the entirety of the submerged chopstick, the oil is ready.

Prepare a wire rack over a baking sheet and place next to the stove.

Use tongs to carefully lower each wrapped shrimp into the hot oil. Work in batches and do not overcrowd the pan. Fry each shrimp until the noodles are golden brown, turning occasionally, about 2 to 3 minutes in total. Remove the fried shrimp to the wire rack and repeat with remaining shrimp.

Plate a small pond of passion-coconut sauce topped with several fried shrimp for serving.

"They were hungry for breakfast which they ate at the cafe, ordering brioche and cafe au lait and eggs, and the type of preserve that they chose and the manner in which the eggs were to be cooked was an excitement."

—THE GARDEN OF EDEN

TORTILLA VAGA DE BACALAO

Salt-Cod "Lazy" Spanish Tortilla

TOTAL TIME: 15 minutes, plus 36 hours to desalt the cod

SERVES: 3 to 4 as a tapa or an appetizer, 2 to 3 as an entrée

The "lazy" *tortilla vaga* was invented in Madrid at Restaurante Sacha by Chef Sacha Hormaechea with one simple goal: To allow the starring ingredients to be consumed by all the senses before eating, as only an open-topped egg concoction can. "Like a pizza, but with eggs," affirms Chef Sacha. Given the trend toward ingredient-forward cooking across Spain, this concept spread like wildfire.

4 ounces salt-cod fillet

3 tablespoons extra-virgin olive oil

6 large eggs

½ teaspoon kosher salt

1 roasted red bell pepper, peeled, seeded, and diced

1 tablespoon minced parsley

Under cold running water, rinse the exterior salt from the salt-cod. In a large bowl, cover the salt-cod with more cold water, cover, and refrigerate for 36 hours, replacing the water 3 times through the duration.

Preheat the oven to 375°F.

Remove the salt-cod from the refrigerator, discard the water, rinse and dry the fish on paper towels. Coat the cod with 1 tablespoon of olive oil and place it on a baking sheet, if it has skin, skin-side down. Transfer the baking sheet to the oven and roast for 10 minutes. Remove the salt-cod from the oven and use a fork to remove the skin. Use a fork or two to flake the fish and set aside.

In a mixing bowl, whisk the eggs with salt. Add the remaining 2 tablespoons of olive oil to an 8-inch nonstick skillet over medium-low heat. When the oil begins to shimmer, pour the egg mixture into the skillet and use a rubber spatula to occasionally move the egg mixture around as it cooks for the first 2 minutes, gently redistributing cooked curds from the bottom and ensuring a balanced circle. Allow the bottom and sides of the *tortilla* to cook undisturbed for 1 minute. Swirl the pan to assure the bottom is fully cooked and not sticking.

Place flakes of salt-cod across the top of the eggs, followed by the diced peppers. Turn off the heat and cover the skillet for 2 minutes, until the egg is mostly cooked.

Slide the *tortilla vaga* onto a plate, garnish with parsley, and dig in.

NOTE ABOUT SALT-COD: *As a substitute, you may use fresh cod that has been seasoned with 1 teaspoon of kosher salt for every 1 pound of fish and set aside for 1 hour. In this case, skip the soaking and rinsing steps and simply use the seasoned fresh fish in the recipe. The texture will not be as meaty as salt-cod, but the overall effect is maintained.*

"I'd better stick to writing."

—Hemingway's Response to Trying His Hand at Cooking Paella at Sobrino de Botín in Madrid

GALLETAS DE SOCARRAT
Crispy Rice Cookies

TOTAL TIME: 1 hour, plus overnight, plus 15 minutes
SERVES: 5 to 10 as a tapa or an appetizer

Socarrat is the prize of any *arróz seco*, or dry-rice dish, of which paella is the prime example. The thin, even layer of toasted rice that sits on the bottom of the pan is technical, hard to achieve, and a crispy treat for diners while in the hands of an excellent cook. This dish is all prize, and easier to achieve.

4 tablespoons extra-virgin olive oil, divided

½ cup tomato purée

2 cloves garlic, minced

2 teaspoons smoke paprika

½ teaspoon kosher salt

1 pinch saffron threads

1 cup uncooked Spanish round rice, such as *bomba* or *calasparra*

3 cups chicken or vegetable stock

1 egg yolk

¼ cup *Alioli Clásico* from *Patatas Bravas* (page 171)

6 to 8 pickled red chiles, drained

2 tablespoons fresh oregano leaves

1 teaspoon capers, drained (optional)

First, cook the rice as for paella: Preheat the oven to 350°F. Add 2 tablespoons of olive oil to a *paellera* or oven-safe skillet over medium-high heat. When the oil begins to shimmer, add the tomato purée, garlic, paprika, salt, and saffron and sauté for 3 to 4 minutes, until the tomato has mostly dried. Stir in the rice until each grain has been coated with the tomato mixture. Carefully pour in the stock and stir until the rice is evenly distributed in the pan. Transfer the pan to the oven and braise for 30 to 35 minutes, until all the liquid has been absorbed.

Remove rice from the oven and allow it to cool for at least 25 minutes. In a mixing bowl, evenly blend the egg yolk into the cooked rice, cover and refrigerate overnight.

Remove the rice from the refrigerator and form into at least 5 balls, then into ½-inch-thick disks. Add the remaining 2 tablespoons of olive oil to a skillet over medium heat. When the oil begins to shimmer, add a few disks to the oil. Work in batches if necessary and do not overcrowd the pan. Fry the disks for 2 to 3 minutes per side, until golden brown. Set aside to drain.

Serve the "cookies" hot topped with *alioli clásico*, pickled peppers, oregano, and capers, if using.

"The truly brave bull gives no warning before he charges except the fixing of his eye on his enemy, the raising of the crest of muscle in his neck, the twitching of an ear, and, as he charges, the lifting of his tail."

—*Death in the Afternoon*

TATIN DE RABO DE BUEY
Oxtail Puff Pastry

TOTAL TIME: 1 hour
SERVES: 3 to 5 as a tapa or an appetizer

Estofado de rabo de toro, oxtail stew, is as traditional as traditional gets across Spain, and chefs still strive to perfect the dish in its purest form. However, we've seen very creative interpretations of late. Baserriberri in Pamplona has its *ressandwich*, a shrimp-toastlike treatment. Karak in Valencia offers the stew in a ramen bowl. But, this *tatín* from A Restaurant in the Hotel Neri in Barcelona captured our imagination.

8 to 10 ounces leftover meat from *Rabo de Toro* (page 62), shredded

2 to 3 ounces leftover sauce from *Rabo de Toro* (page 62)

1 tablespoon plus 1 teaspoon extra-virgin olive oil, divided

1 large golden or other tart apple, peeled, cored, and cut into 6 wedges

½ sheet puff pastry, thawed, rolled out to 4 by 10-inches

1 large egg, whisked with 1 tablespoon water

Fresh rosemary sprigs, for garnish

Preheat the oven to 350°F.

In a mixing bowl, add 1 tablespoon at a time of leftover sauce to the shredded beef until you can form a ball without it falling apart. Place a 12-by-12-inch sheet of plastic wrap over a baking sheet, and on the plastic, press to form a rough 3-by-10-inch rectangle of shredded beef, no more than ½ inch thick. Use the plastic wrap to straighten the edges of the rectangle, so the beef is encased in plastic. Place the baking sheet with the wrapped beef on top in the freezer for 30 minutes.

On a separate baking sheet, brush a layer of olive oil and place the slices of apple. Brush the tops of the slices with additional olive oil, transfer to the oven, and roast for 30 minutes. Remove the apples and reset the oven to 400°F. In a glass container, use an immersion blender to purée 1 apple slice with 1 teaspoon of olive oil and set aside.

Wipe the baking sheet clean and place the puff pastry sheet on the sheet. Dock the pastry with a fork evenly about 12 times. Brush the top of the pastry with egg wash. Remove the beef rectangle from the freezer, unwrap, and place along one 10-inch edge of the puff pastry. Brush the top of the beef lightly with additional *rabo de toro* sauce. Top the beef with 5 slices of par-roasted apples and brush the apples with the same sauce. Transfer to the oven and bake for 15 to 20 minutes, until the pastry has browned and crisped.

Remove the *tatín* from the oven and transfer to a platter. Dollop the exposed pastry with apple purée and garnish each dollop with fresh rosemary. Serve warm.

"An Explanatory Glossary of Certain Words, Terms, and Phrases"

—*Death in the Afternoon*

Aficionado: one passionate about bullfights

Ahumada: smoked

Ajillo: seasoned with garlic

Ajo: garlic

Albóndigas: meatball

Alcachofa: artichoke

Aliñada: seasoned

Almeja: clam

Alubia: white bean

Anguila: eel

Arróz: rice

Asada/o: roasted

Atún: tuna

Avellana: hazelnut

Bacalao: salt-cured cod

Berenjena: eggplant

Blanco: white

Bocadillo: sandwich

Brava: brave, ferocious, angry

Carrillera: beef or pork cheeks

Carta: menu

Cebolla: onion

Cecina: salt-cured and air-dried beef

Chivito: young goat

Chorizo: spiced, cured, and dried sausage

Cochinillo: suckling pig

Cocido: stew

Confitado/s: oil-poached

Cordero: lamb

Corrida: bullfight

Cremaet: burnt rum and coffee

Croqueta: croquette

Empanadilla: turnover, hand pie

Encierro: running of the bulls

Encurtida: pickled

Ensalada: salad

Ensaladilla: small salad

Escabechada: poached in highly acidic liquid

Espinacas: spinach

Fiesta: party, festival

Flamenquín: chicken roulade

Fideo: noodle

Frito/a: fried

Fritura: fried snack

Galleta: cookie

Gamba: shrimp

Garbanzo: chickpea

Gazpacho: chilled vegetable soup

Glaseado/a: glazed

Hongo: wild mushroom

Horchata: chilled tiger-nut milk

Huevo: egg

Jamón: salt-cured and air-dried pork leg

Langostino: large shrimp

Lomo alto: New York strip steak

Madrileño/a: resident or emblematic of Madrid

Marisco: seafood

Miel de caña: molasses

Miga: crumb

Mojama: salt-cured tuna

Morcilla: blood sausage, black pudding

Paella de mariscos: seafood rice

Paella Valenciana: chicken and rabbit rice

Pan: bread

Papa: potato

Parrilla: grill

Parrillada: grilled

Patata: potato

Pato: duck

Perdiz: partridge

Pescado: fish

Pimiento: pepper, chile

Pimiento del padrón: green pepper from Galicia

Pimiento del piquillo: red pepper from Navarra

Pintxo: canapé

Pisto: ratatouille

Postre: dessert

Pundonor: honor, probity, courage, self-respect, pride

Queso Manchego: aged cheese from La Mancha

Rabo de toro: oxtail

Relleno/a: stuffed

Revuelto/a: scrambled

Riojana: from Rioja

Rojo: red

Salmonete: red mullet fish

Salmorejo: chilled tomato soup

Sangría: fruit-infused wine

Sevillano/a: resident or emblematic of Sevilla

Socarrat: crispy rice, bottom of paella

Soja: soy

Solomillo: tenderloin

Sopa: soup

Tapa: cover, small plate

Tapeo: the act of eating tapas

Tarta: cake

Temporada: seasonal

Tomates: tomatoes

Toro: bull

Torrija: French toast

Tortilla Española: egg and potato cake

Trucha: trout

Trufado: truffled

Tuetano: bone marrow

Vaca madurada: dry-aged beef

Valenciano/a: resident or emblematic of Valencia

Verano: summer

Vermút casera: house-made vermouth, fortified wine

Viaje: journey

Vino tinto: red wine

Yema: yolk

ERNEST HEMINGWAY'S SPAIN

a Timeline

1921	First visit to Spain, a stopover in the port at Vigo en route to Paris.
1923	First visit to Pamplona on the advice of Gertrude Stein to see the Running of the Bulls during the *Fiesta de San Fermín*.
1924	Return to Pamplona for the bullfights and fishing in the Pyrenees.
1925	Another visit to Pamplona for the bulls, with trips to San Sebastián, Madrid, and Valencia, where he begins to write *The Sun Also Rises*.
1926 TO 1933	Summers watching bullfights; culminates in *Death in the Afternoon*.
1934	Summer in Spain watching bullfights, en route to Kenya to begin research for *Green Hills of Africa*.
1935	Summer for bullfights; writes "Notes on the Next War" for *Esquire* magazine; displays a keen sense of growing tensions in Europe.
1936	Summer for bullfights; the Spanish Civil War breaks out in July, which draws his journalistic curiosity.
1937 TO 1938	War reporting for the North American Newspaper Alliance; stationed in Madrid with trips to Valencia, Barcelona, and the front lines. Helps produce the documentary *The Spanish Earth* and briefly joins the fight with the International Brigade. All of which informs the writing of *For Whom the Bell Tolls.*
1939 TO 1952	Whether self-imposed exile or persona non grata in Spain, Hemingway eventually lobbies for a negotiated return.
1953	Return to Pamplona for the *Fiesta de San Fermín*.
1954 TO 1959	Many visits to various parts of Spain gathering material for a *Life* magazine series that is compiled to become *The Dangerous Summer*.
1960	Hemingway's final visit to Spain.

INDEX

A

aioli
about, 25
in Galletas de Socarrat (Crispy Rice Cookies), 189
Garlic-Lemon Aioli, 36
Quick Aioli, 106
Ajo Blanco (Chilled White Garlic Soup), 95
Albóndigas al Curry Rojo (Meatballs in Red Curry), 120
Alcachofas Parrilladas (Grilled Artichokes), 69
Alioli Clásico, 171
Almejas con Chorizo (Clams with Sausage), 112
almond flour
Tarta de Santiago (Almond Flour Cake), 33
almonds
Ajo Blanco (Chilled White Garlic Soup), 95
Roasted Almonds, 155
White Garlic Sauce, 44
anchovy fillets
Pintxo de Gilda (Skewer of Olive, Pepper, and Anchovy), 178
apples
Tatin de Rabo de Buey (Oxtail Puff Pastry), 191
Arróz de Vaca Madurada (Dry-Aged Beef Rice), 128
Arróz del Senyoret con Salmonete (Naked Seafood and Fish Rice), 114–115
artichokes
Alcachofas Parrilladas (Grilled Artichokes), 69

B

Bacalao con Tomate (Salt-Cod in Tomato Sauce), 89
bacalao method, 22
bacon
El Chivito (Pork, Bacon, and Egg Sandwich), 135
Migas de Pastor con Chistorra (Breadcrumbs, Fried Egg, and Sausage), 143–144
banana peppers
Pintxo de Gilda (Skewer of Olive, Pepper, and Anchovy), 178
Barcelona, 184–185
Béarnaise Sauce, 163
beef
Albóndigas al Curry Rojo (Meatballs in Red Curry), 120
Arróz de Vaca Madurada (Dry-Aged Beef Rice), 128
cheeks, 25
Lomo Alto a la Parrilla (Grilled New York Strip Steak), 168
Pimientos Rellenos (Stuffed Roasted Peppers), 127
Tartar de Toro con Tuetano (Beef Tartare with Bone Marrow), 92
beef marrow bone
Tartar de Toro con Tuetano (Beef Tartare with Bone Marrow), 92
beer
Almejas con Chorizo (Clams with Sausage), 112
bell peppers
Albóndigas al Curry Rojo (Meatballs in Red Curry), 120
Bocadillo de Morcilla y Revueltos (Black Sausage and Egg Sandwich), 122
Empanadilla de Atún (Tuna Turnover), 136
Gazpacho (Chilled Vegetable Soup), 67
Patatas a la Riojana (Rioja Potato Stew), 165
Pickled Peppers, 122
Tortilla Vaga de Bacalao (Salt-Cod "Lazy" Spanish Tortilla), 188
Berenjenas con Miel de Caña (Fried Eggplant with Molasses), 74
Berenjenas con Soja y Miso (Eggplant with Soy and Miso), 119
blood sausage
about, 25
Bocadillo de Morcilla y Revueltos (Black Sausage and Egg Sandwich), 122
Bocadillo de Calamares (Fried Squid Sandwich), 36
Bocadillo de Morcilla y Revueltos (Black Sausage and Egg Sandwich), 122
bomba rice
about, 25
Arróz de Vaca Madurada (Dry-Aged Beef Rice), 128
Arróz del Senyoret con Salmonete (Naked Seafood and Fish Rice), 114–115
Galletas de Socarrat (Crispy Rice Cookies), 189
Paella Valenciana (Chicken and Rabbit Rice), 109
Boomveja! Pintxo de Cordero (Shredded Lamb Canapé), 158–159
brandy
Sangría (Fruit-Infused Wine), 110
Vermút Casera (House-Made Fortified Wine), 145
bread
in Albóndigas al Curry Rojo (Meatballs in Red Curry), 120
in Bocadillo de Calamares (Fried Squid Sandwich), 36
in Bocadillo de Morcilla y Revueltos (Black Sausage and Egg Sandwich), 122
Coca de Berenjena y Tomate (Tomato and Eggplant Flatbread), 132
in El Chivito (Pork, Bacon, and Egg Sandwich), 135
in Gazpacho (Chilled Vegetable Soup), 67
in Migas de Pastor con Chistorra (Breadcrumbs, Fried Egg, and Sausage), 143–144
in Pan con Tomate (Toast with Tomato Sauce), 81
in Pimientos Rellenos (Stuffed Roasted Peppers), 127
in Pintxo de Anguila y Tomate (Eel and Tomato Canapé), 156
in Salmorejo (Chilled Tomato Soup), 85
in Sopa de Ajo (Garlic Soup), 35
in Torrijas (French Toast), 86
in Tosta con Mantequilla y Mermelada (Raspberry Jam on Toast), 162
in White Garlic Sauce, 44
breadcrumbs
Croquetas de Jamón (Ham Croquettes), 47
Flamenquín (Chicken Roulade), 78
Migas de Pastor con Chistorra (Breadcrumbs, Fried Egg, and Sausage), 143–144
butter beans
Paella Valenciana (Chicken and Rabbit Rice), 109

C

cabbage
Ensaladilla de Albuias (White Bean Salad), 148
cakes
Tarta de Queso (Basque "Burnt" Cheesecake), 183
Tarta de Santiago (Almond Flour Cake), 33

Carrilleras con Pimientos Cristal (Braised Pork Cheeks and Peppers), 177
cheese
El Chivito (Pork, Bacon, and Egg Sandwich), 135
Flamenquín (Chicken Roulade), 78
Queso Manchego con Miel y Avellanas (Manchego Cheese with Honey and Hazelnuts), 40
Tapa Bretón (Roasted Goat Cheese), 54
chicken
Flamenquín (Chicken Roulade), 78
Paella Valenciana (Chicken and Rabbit Rice), 109
chickpeas
Espinacas con Garbanzos (Spinach and Chickpeas), 77
chistorra
about, 25
Migas de Pastor con Chistorra (Breadcrumbs, Fried Egg, and Sausage), 143–144
Chorizo al Vino (Red Wine Chorizo), 43
Chuletas de Cordero a la Parrilla (Grilled Lamb Chops), 101
Cilantro Oil, 54
cinnamon
Cremaet (Burnt Rum Coffee), 123
Horchata (Chilled Tiger-Nut Milk), 133
Tomato-Cinnamon *Mermelada*, 54
clams
Almejas con Chorizo (Clams with Sausage), 112
"A Clean, Well-Lighted Place," 82
Coca de Berenjena y Tomate (Tomato and Eggplant Flatbread), 132
Cochinillo Asado con Patatas Asadas (Roasted Suckling Pig and Potatoes), 32
cocktails
Cremaet (Burnt Rum Coffee), 123
Papa Doble (Hemingway Daiquiri), 41
Sangría (Fruit-Infused Wine), 110
Tinto de Verano (Red Wine Spritzer), 56
Vermút Casera (House-Made Fortified Wine), 145
coconut cream
Passion-Coconut Sauce, 186
coconut milk
Ajo Blanco (Chilled White Garlic Soup), 95
Albóndigas al Curry Rojo (Meatballs in Red Curry), 120
cod. *See* salt-cod
coffee
Cremaet (Burnt Rum Coffee), 123
condiments
Cilantro Oil, 54
Garlic-Lemon Aioli, 36
Pickled Peppers, 122
Quick Aioli, 106
Raspberry Jam, 162
Tomato-Cinnamon *Mermelada*, 54
Confit de Pato Glaseado (Glazed Duck Confit), 59
corn
Ensalada de Perdiz Escabechada (Poached Partridge with Salad), 180
crayfish tails
Pimientos Rellenos (Stuffed Roasted Peppers), 127
cream
Cremaet (Burnt Rum Coffee), 123
Tarta de Queso (Basque "Burnt" Cheesecake), 183
cream cheese
Pimientos Rellenos (Stuffed Roasted Peppers), 127
Tarta de Queso (Basque "Burnt" Cheesecake), 183
Cremaet (Burnt Rum Coffee), 123
Croquetas de Jamón (Ham Croquettes), 47
cucumbers
Gazpacho (Chilled Vegetable Soup), 67
curry paste
Albóndigas al Curry Rojo (Meatballs in Red Curry), 120

D

The Dangerous Summer, 18, 66, 70, 90, 104, 116
Death in the Afternoon, 18, 30, 38, 52, 60, 80, 96, 124, 184
drinks. *See also* cocktails
Horchata (Chilled Tiger-Nut Milk), 133
duck
Confit de Pato Glaseado (Glazed Duck Confit), 59

E

eel fillets
Pintxo de Anguila y Tomate (Eel and Tomato Canapé), 156
eggplant
Berenjenas con Miel de Caña (Fried Eggplant with Molasses), 74
Berenjenas con Soja y Miso (Eggplant with Soy and Miso), 119
Coca de Berenjena y Tomate (Tomato and Eggplant Flatbread), 132
Pisto (Ratatouille), 174
eggs
Alioli Clásico, 171
Bocadillo de Morcilla y Revueltos (Black Sausage and Egg Sandwich), 122
El Chivito (Pork, Bacon, and Egg Sandwich), 135
Garlic-Lemon Aioli, 36
Hongos de Temporada y Yema (Seasonal Mushrooms with Egg Yolk), 44
Huevo Trufado (Truffled Egg), 153
Migas de Pastor con Chistorra (Breadcrumbs, Fried Egg, and Sausage), 143–144
Papas Aliñadas (Potato Salad), 72
Revueltos de Hongos (Scrambled Eggs with Mushrooms), 179
Salmon and Mango Tartare, 163
Salmorejo (Chilled Tomato Soup), 85
Sopa de Ajo (Garlic Soup), 35
Torrijas (French Toast), 86
Tortilla Española de Patatas (Spanish Potato Tortilla), 50–51
Tortilla Vaga de Bacalao (Salt-Cod "Lazy" Spanish Tortilla), 188
El Chivito (Pork, Bacon, and Egg Sandwich), 135
Empanadilla de Atún (Tuna Turnover), 136
Ensalada de Perdiz Escabechada (Poached Partridge with Salad), 180
Ensaladilla de Albuias (White Bean Salad), 148
Espinacas con Garbanzos (Spinach and Chickpeas), 77
espresso
Cremaet (Burnt Rum Coffee), 123
extra-virgin olive oil, about, 25

F

fish
Arróz del Senyoret con Salmonete (Naked Seafood and Fish Rice), 114–115
Bacalao con Tomate (Salt-Cod in Tomato Sauce), 89
Empanadilla de Atún (Tuna Turnover), 136
Fish Stock, 114
Mojama con Cebollas Encurtidas (Salt-Cured Tuna and Pickled Onions), 155
Papas Aliñadas (Potato Salad), 72
room temperature cooking, 22
Salmon and Mango Tartare, 95
Salmón con Salsa Béarnaise (Broiled Salmon with Béarnaise Sauce), 163
Tataki de Atún (Seared Ahi Tuna), 106

Tortilla Vaga de Bacalao (Salt-Cod "Lazy" Spanish Tortilla), 188
Trucha Ahumada (Smoked Trout), 147
Flamenquín (Chicken Roulade), 78
For Whom the Bell Tolls, 18, 48, 52, 70, 71, 80, 116, 117, 130, 150, 167, 184
French fries
Huevo Trufado (Truffled Egg), 153

G

Galletas de Socarrat (Crispy Rice Cookies), 189
Gambas al Ajillo (Sizzling Garlic Shrimp), 98
garlic
Ajo Blanco (Chilled White Garlic Soup), 95
Gambas al Ajillo (Sizzling Garlic Shrimp), 98
Garlic-Lemon Aioli, 36
Sopa de Ajo (Garlic Soup), 35
White Garlic Sauce, 44
Gazpacho (Chilled Vegetable Soup), 67
goat cheese
El Chivito (Pork, Bacon, and Egg Sandwich), 135
Tapa Bretón (Roasted Goat Cheese), 54
grapefruit juice
Papa Doble (Hemingway Daiquiri), 41
green beans
Ensaladilla de Albuias (White Bean Salad), 148
Paella Valenciana (Chicken and Rabbit Rice), 109

H

hazelnuts
Queso Manchego con Miel y Avellanas (Manchego Cheese with Honey and Hazelnuts), 40
honey
Queso Manchego con Miel y Avellanas (Manchego Cheese with Honey and Hazelnuts), 40
Tosta con Mantequilla y Mermelada (Raspberry Jam on Toast), 162
Hongos de Temporada y Yema (Seasonal Mushrooms with Egg Yolk), 44
Horchata (Chilled Tiger-Nut Milk), 133
Huevo Trufado (Truffled Egg), 153

I

ingredients, 25

L

lamb
Chuletas de Cordero a la Parrilla (Grilled Lamb Chops), 101
Pintxo de Anguila y Tomate (Eel and Tomato Canapé), 158–159
Langostino Wonton (Fried Shrimp in Noodles), 186
lemons
Garlic-Lemon Aioli, 36
Sangría (Fruit-Infused Wine), 110
Vermút Casera (House-Made Fortified Wine), 145
limes
Papa Doble (Hemingway Daiquiri), 41
Lomo Alto a la Parrilla (Grilled New York Strip Steak), 168

M

Madrid, 30–31, 38–39, 48–49, 52–53, 60–61
Manchego cheese
Queso Manchego con Miel y Avellanas (Manchego Cheese with Honey and Hazelnuts), 40
mangos
Salmon and Mango Tartare, 95
maraschino liqueur
Papa Doble (Hemingway Daiquiri), 41
Meatballs, 120
Migas de Pastor con Chistorra (Breadcrumbs, Fried Egg, and Sausage), 143–144
milk
Torrijas (French Toast), 86
Truffle Cream, 153
Truffled Béchamel, 153
miso paste
Berenjenas con Soja y Miso (Eggplant with Soy and Miso), 119
Mojama con Cebollas Encurtidas (Salt-Cured Tuna and Pickled Onions), 155
molasses
Berenjenas con Miel de Caña (Fried Eggplant with Molasses), 74
mushrooms
Hongos de Temporada y Yema (Seasonal Mushrooms with Egg Yolk), 44
Revueltos de Hongos (Scrambled Eggs with Mushrooms), 179

N

noodles
Langostino Wonton (Fried Shrimp in Noodles), 186

O

The Old Man and the Sea, 82, 104
olives
Pintxo de Anguila y Tomate (Eel and Tomato Canapé), 156
Pintxo de Gilda (Skewer of Olive, Pepper, and Anchovy), 178
onions
Mojama con Cebollas Encurtidas (Salt-Cured Tuna and Pickled Onions), 155
Pickled Red Onion, 155
oranges
Sangría (Fruit-Infused Wine), 110
Vermút Casera (House-Made Fortified Wine), 145
oxtails
Rabo de Toro (Braised Oxtail), 62
Tatin de Rabo de Buey (Oxtail Puff Pastry), 191

P

padrón peppers
about, 25
Pimientos del Padrón Fritos (Blistered Padrón Peppers), 97
paella, about, 22
Paella Valenciana (Chicken and Rabbit Rice), 109
Pamplona, 140–141, 146, 150–152, 160–161, 166–167, 172–173
Pan con Tomate (Toast with Tomato Sauce), 81
Pancakes, 158
Papa Doble (Hemingway Daiquiri), 41
Papas Aliñadas (Potato Salad), 72
partridge
about, 25
Ensalada de Perdiz Escabechada (Poached Partridge with Salad), 180
Passion-Coconut Sauce, 186
Patatas a la Riojana (Rioja Potato Stew), 165
Patatas Bravas (Roasted Potatoes with "Brave" Sauce), 171
peas
Ensaladilla de Albuias (White Bean Salad), 148
peppers. *See* banana peppers; bell peppers; *padrón* peppers; *piquillo* peppers
Pickled Peppers, 122
Pickled Red Onion, 155
Pimientos del Padrón Fritos (Blistered Padrón Peppers), 97
Pimientos del Piquillo Confitados (Charred Roasted Peppers), 111

in Carrilleras con Pimientos Cristal (Braised Pork Cheeks and Peppers), 177
Pimientos Rellenos (Stuffed Roasted Peppers), 127
pine nuts
Coca de Berenjena y Tomate (Tomato and Eggplant Flatbread), 132
Pintxo de Anguila y Tomate (Eel and Tomato Canapé), 156
Pintxo de Gilda (Skewer of Olive, Pepper, and Anchovy), 178
pintxos, about, 22
piquillo peppers
about, 25
Carrilleras con Pimientos Cristal (Braised Pork Cheeks and Peppers), 177
Lomo Alto a la Parrilla (Grilled New York Strip Steak), 168
Pimientos del Piquillo Confitados (Charred Roasted Peppers), 111
Pimientos Rellenos (Stuffed Roasted Peppers), 127
Pisto (Ratatouille), 174
Salsa Brava, 171
Pisto (Ratatouille), 174
pork. *See also* bacon; sausage; Spanish ham; suckling pig
Albóndigas al Curry Rojo (Meatballs in Red Curry), 120
Carrilleras con Pimientos Cristal (Braised Pork Cheeks and Peppers), 177
cheeks, 25
El Chivito (Pork, Bacon, and Egg Sandwich), 135
Solomillo al Whiskey (Pork Tenderloin with Whiskey Sauce), 75
port
Confit de Pato Glaseado (Glazed Duck Confit), 59
potatoes
Cochinillo Asado con Patatas Asadas (Roasted Suckling Pig and Potatoes), 32
Papas Aliñadas (Potato Salad), 72
Patatas a la Riojana (Rioja Potato Stew), 165
Patatas Bravas (Roasted Potatoes with "Brave" Sauce), 171
Tortilla Española de Patatas (Spanish Potato Tortilla), 50–51
prune juice
Confit de Pato Glaseado (Glazed Duck Confit), 59
puff pastry
Tatin de Rabo de Buey (Oxtail Puff Pastry), 191

Q

Queso Manchego con Miel y Avellanas (Manchego Cheese with Honey and Hazelnuts), 40
Quick Aioli, 106

R

rabbit meat
about, 25
Paella Valenciana (Chicken and Rabbit Rice), 109
Rabo de Toro (Braised Oxtail), 62
in Tatin de Rabo de Buey (Oxtail Puff Pastry), 191
raspberries
Tosta con Mantequilla y Mermelada (Raspberry Jam on Toast), 162
red chiles, pickled
Galletas de Socarrat (Crispy Rice Cookies), 189
Red Curry Sauce, 120
Revueltos de Hongos (Scrambled Eggs with Mushrooms), 179
rice. *See bomba* rice
Roasted Almonds, 155
rum
Cremaet (Burnt Rum Coffee), 123
Papa Doble (Hemingway Daiquiri), 41

S

saffron
about, 25
Arróz de Vaca Madurada (Dry-Aged Beef Rice), 128
Arróz del Senyoret con Salmonete (Naked Seafood and Fish Rice), 114
Galletas de Socarrat (Crispy Rice Cookies), 189
Paella Valenciana (Chicken and Rabbit Rice), 109
salads
Ensalada de Perdiz Escabechada (Poached Partridge with Salad), 180
Ensaladilla de Albuias (White Bean Salad), 148
Papas Aliñadas (Potato Salad), 72
salmon
Salmon and Mango Tartare, 95
Salmón con Salsa Béarnaise (Broiled Salmon with Béarnaise Sauce), 163
Salmón con Salsa Béarnaise (Broiled Salmon with Béarnaise Sauce), 163
Salmorejo (Chilled Tomato Soup), 85
Salsa Brava, 171
salt-cod
about, 22, 25
Bacalao con Tomate (Salt-Cod in Tomato Sauce), 89
Tortilla Vaga de Bacalao (Salt-Cod "Lazy" Spanish Tortilla), 188
sandwiches
Bocadillo de Calamares (Fried Squid Sandwich), 36
Bocadillo de Morcilla y Revueltos (Black Sausage and Egg Sandwich), 122
El Chivito (Pork, Bacon, and Egg Sandwich), 135
Pan con Tomate (Toast with Tomato Sauce), 81
Tosta con Mantequilla y Mermelada (Raspberry Jam on Toast), 162
Sangría (Fruit-Infused Wine), 110
sauces. *See also* aioli
Béarnaise Sauce, 163
Passion-Coconut Sauce, 186
Red Curry Sauce, 120
Salsa Brava, 171
Sweet Soy Sauce, 106
Tomato-Caramel Sauce, 78
Truffle Cream, 153, 159
Truffled Béchamel, 153
White Garlic Sauce, 44
sausage
Almejas con Chorizo (Clams with Sausage), 112
blood sausage, 25
Bocadillo de Morcilla y Revueltos (Black Sausage and Egg Sandwich), 122
chistorra, 25
Chorizo al Vino (Red Wine Chorizo), 43
Patatas a la Riojana (Rioja Potato Stew), 165
Spanish chorizo, 25
seafood. *See also* fish
Almejas con Chorizo (Clams with Sausage), 112
Gambas al Ajillo (Sizzling Garlic Shrimp), 98
Langostino Wonton (Fried Shrimp in Noodles), 186
room temperature cooking, 22
Sevilla, 66, 70–71, 80, 82–83, 90–91, 96
sherry
Vermút Casera (House-Made Fortified Wine), 145

shrimp
Fish Stock, 114
Gambas al Ajillo (Sizzling Garlic Shrimp), 98
Langostino Wonton (Fried Shrimp in Noodles), 186
smoked paprika, about, 25
soda
Tinto de Verano (Red Wine Spritzer), 56
Solomillo al Whiskey (Pork Tenderloin with Whiskey Sauce), 75
Sopa de Ajo (Garlic Soup), 35
soups and stews
Ajo Blanco (Chilled White Garlic Soup), 95
Gazpacho (Chilled Vegetable Soup), 67
Patatas a la Riojana (Rioja Potato Stew), 165
Pisto (Ratatouille), 174
Salmorejo (Chilled Tomato Soup), 85
Sopa de Ajo (Garlic Soup), 35
soy sauce
Berenjenas con Soja y Miso (Eggplant with Soy and Miso), 119
Sweet Soy Sauce, 106
Spanish chorizo
about, 25
Almejas con Chorizo (Clams with Sausage), 112
Chorizo al Vino (Red Wine Chorizo), 43
Patatas a la Riojana (Rioja Potato Stew), 165
Spanish ham
about, 25
Alcachofas Parrilladas (Grilled Artichokes), 69
Croquetas de Jamón (Ham Croquettes), 47
Ensaladilla de Albuias (White Bean Salad), 148
Flamenquín (Chicken Roulade), 78
Gazpacho (Chilled Vegetable Soup), 67
Huevo Trufado (Truffled Egg), 153
Salmorejo (Chilled Tomato Soup), 85
Sopa de Ajo (Garlic Soup), 35
spinach
Coca de Berenjena y Tomate (Tomato and Eggplant Flatbread), 132
Espinacas con Garbanzos (Spinach and Chickpeas), 77
squid
Arróz del Senyoret con Salmonete (Naked Seafood and Fish Rice), 114–115
Bocadillo de Calamares (Fried Squid Sandwich), 36
substitutions, 25
suckling pig
about, 25
Cochinillo Asado con Patatas Asadas (Roasted Suckling Pig and Potatoes), 32
The Sun Also Rises, 18, 19, 30, 32, 60, 104, 140, 146, 150, 160, 166, 172
Sweet Soy Sauce, 106

T

Tapa Bretón (Roasted Goat Cheese), 54
tapas, about, 22
Tarta de Queso (Basque "Burnt" Cheesecake), 183
Tarta de Santiago (Almond Flour Cake), 33
Tartar de Toro con Tuetano (Beef Tartare with Bone Marrow), 92
Tataki de Atún (Seared Ahi Tuna), 106
Tatin de Rabo de Buey (Oxtail Puff Pastry), 191
tiger nuts
Horchata (Chilled Tiger-Nut Milk), 133
Tinto de Verano (Red Wine Spritzer), 56
Tomates Aliñados (Dressed Tomatoes), 57
tomatoes
Bacalao con Tomate (Salt-Cod in Tomato Sauce), 89
Coca de Berenjena y Tomate (Tomato and Eggplant Flatbread), 132
El Chivito (Pork, Bacon, and Egg Sandwich), 135
Ensalada de Perdiz Escabechada (Poached Partridge with Salad), 180
Gazpacho (Chilled Vegetable Soup), 67
grating, 23
Migas de Pastor con Chistorra (Breadcrumbs, Fried Egg, and Sausage), 143–144
Paella Valenciana (Chicken and Rabbit Rice), 109
Pan con Tomate (Toast with Tomato Sauce), 81
Pisto (Ratatouille), 174
Salmorejo (Chilled Tomato Soup), 85
Tomates Aliñados (Dressed Tomatoes), 57
Tomato-Caramel Sauce, 78
Tomato-Cinnamon *Mermelada*, 54
Torrijas (French Toast), 86
Tortilla Española de Patatas (Spanish Potato Tortilla), 50–51
Tortilla Vaga de Bacalao (Salt-Cod "Lazy" Spanish Tortilla), 188
tortillas, about, 23
Tosta con Mantequilla y Mermelada (Raspberry Jam on Toast), 162
trout
Trucha Ahumada (Smoked Trout), 147
Trucha Ahumada (Smoked Trout), 147
Truffle Cream, 153, 159
Truffled Béchamel, 153
tuna
Empanadilla de Atún (Tuna Turnover), 136
Mojama con Cebollas Encurtidas (Salt-Cured Tuna and Pickled Onions), 155
Papas Aliñadas (Potato Salad), 72
Tataki de Atún (Seared Ahi Tuna), 106

V

Valencia, 104–105, 116–117, 124–125, 130–131
vermouth
Tinto de Verano (Red Wine Spritzer), 56
Vermút Casera (House-Made Fortified Wine), 145

W

whiskey
Solomillo al Whiskey (Pork Tenderloin with Whiskey Sauce), 75
white beans
Ensaladilla de Albuias (White Bean Salad), 148
White Garlic Sauce, 44
wine, red
Chorizo al Vino (Red Wine Chorizo), 43
Rabo de Toro (Braised Oxtail), 62
Sangría (Fruit-Infused Wine), 110
Tinto de Verano (Red Wine Spritzer), 56
wine, white
Ensalada de Perdiz Escabechada (Poached Partridge with Salad), 180
Salmon and Mango Tartare, 163
Vermút Casera (House-Made Fortified Wine), 145

ABOUT THE AUTHOR

Howie Southworth is a best-selling author and storyteller. His last book, *A Taste of Alexandria: Modern Restaurant Recipes That Echo Our City's Past*, was an ode to his home city. Other past works include *Chinese Street Food: Small Bites, Classic Recipes, and Harrowing Tales Across the Middle Kingdom*; *One Pan to Rule Them All: 100 Cast-Iron Skillet Recipes for Indoors and Out*; *Kiss My Casserole!: 100 Global Recipes for Modern and Easy Oven-Fresh Comfort Foods*; *How to Cook Anything in Your Dutch Oven: Classic American Comfort Foods and New Global Favorites*. He's even written for the *For Dummies* series! Aside from books, Howie has the occasional byline in newspapers and websites. Look for his essay entitled "I drank like Hemingway in Hong Kong" on *Salon*. Outside the written word, Howie has produced food and travel-related media with various creative partners, including Asia Society and restaurant groups in the Washington, DC, Metro Area, Asia, and Europe. In addition to traveling the globe to eat, he and his family have lived in many delicious destinations, from both coasts of the United States to China and Spain. His writing reflects everything he has enjoyed eating and cooking along the way.

weldon**owen**
an imprint of Insight Editions
P.O. Box 3088
San Rafael, CA 94912
www.weldonowen.com

CEO Raoul Goff
VP Publisher Roger Shaw
Executive Editor Edward Ash-Milby
Assistant Editor Kayla Belser
Managing Editor Michelle Hope
Art Director & Designer Megan Sinead Bingham
Production Design Jean Hwang
VP Manufacturing Alix Nicholaeff
Senior Production Manager Joshua Smith
Strategic Production Planner Lina s Palma-Temena

Photography by Stacy Ventura
Food Styling by Victoria Woollard
Food Styling Assistant Allee Cakmis
Prop Styling by Megan Sinead Bingham

Map illustration (page 26) by Chui Kanela

Weldon Owen would also like to thank Margaret Parrish and Dominik Sklarzyk.

ISBN: 979-8-88674-290-9

Manufactured in China by Insight Editions
10 9 8 7 6 5 4 3 2 1

REPLANTED PAPER

Insight Editions, in association with Roots of Peace, will plant two trees for each tree used in the manufacturing of this book. Roots of Peace is an internationally renowned humanitarian organization dedicated to eradicating land mines worldwide and converting war-torn lands into productive farms and wildlife habitats. Roots of Peace will plant two million fruit and nut trees in Afghanistan and provide farmers there with the skills and support necessary for sustainable land use.